NCERT PRACTICE

ENVIRONMENTAL STUDIES

LOOKING AROUND

Manisha Malhotra

ARIHANT PRAKASHAN, MEERUT

WORKBOOK Environmental Studies 5th

Published by Arihant Prakashan, Meerut

卐 **Administrative & Production Offices**

Regd. Office
'Ramchhaya' 4577/15, Agarwal Road, Darya Ganj, New Delhi -110002

Tele: 011- 47630600, 43518550; Fax: 011- 23280316

Head Office
Kalindi, TP Nagar, Meerut (UP) - 250002
Tel: 0121-2401479, 2512970, 4004199; Fax: 0121-2401648

卐 **Sales & Support Offices**

Agra, Ahmedabad, Bengaluru, Bhubaneswar, Bareilly, Chennai, Delhi, Guwahati, Hyderabad, Jaipur, Jhansi, Kolkata, Lucknow, Meerut, Nagpur & Pune.

卐 **ISBN** 978-93-11121-97-0

卐 **Price** ₹ 80.00

Production Team

Publishing Manager
Keshav Mohan, Amit Verma

Project Head
Karishma Yadav

Project Coordinator
Divya Gusain

Project Editor
Gajendra Singh

Cover Designer
Shanu Mansoori

Inner Designer
Ravi Negi

DTP Operator
Vinay Sharma

Proof Readers
Garima Sharma, Pooja Saini

For further information about the books published by Arihant, log on to www.arihantbooks.com or e-mail at info@arihantbooks.com

Workbook, Why?

"Knowledge will not be with you for Long Unless You Practice"

This quotation answer the above question 'Workbook, Why ?'
perfectly, *i.e.,* Workbooks are made to give the students practice required to achieve
perfection and mastery in the subject. These are the only Workbooks, which are strictly
based on **NCERT, the only recommended books by Govt. of India & CBSE**
(reference Circular No. Acad-41/2015 dated 20th July 2015).

Given below is the detailed description of Workbook and some of its special features

ONLY WORKBOOK BASED ON NCERT

NCERT textbooks are the only textbooks, which have been prepared according to
National Curriculum Framework, which discourages the idea of rote learning rather
they focus on understanding and try to make the students able to identify the way of
problem solving.

Keeping the importance of NCERT textbooks in mind we have prepared this Workbook,
strictly based on NCERT content. This Workbook will complement NCERT by providing
practice on the material given in each chapter of NCERT textbook, making the students
understand the chapter completely.

WORKBOOK- PURPOSE, USE & FEATURES

This Workbook, through its **numerous exercises** having different **variety of
questions** covering each and every fact of NCERT, will prove to be **equally useful** for
both, **Classroom** and **at Home**. One more purpose of this Workbook is to provide the
students a **systematic practice** of the content taught in the class and what they study
in the textbooks.

Some special features of this Workbook are

- Complete Coverage of each chapter for complete practice

- Different variety of questions; Fill in the Blanks, True-False, Matching, Multiple
  Choice Questions, Differentiate Between, Define the Following, Very Short
  Answer, Short Answer, Long Answer Type, etc.

- Many questions given in each chapter are related with day-to-day activities
  making them interesting to solve.

- Keeps the students actively engaged with the content and develop enquiry
  skills.

WORKBOOK-DESIGNED TO IMPROVE SUBJECT ABILITIES

All the material given in this Workbook is tailored to suit subject content with equal
support on learning, which will surely help students to boost their abilities and
confidence in the subject.

*I look forward for the feedback from students, teachers and parents for the further improvement of
the contents of this book. I will try to update the contents according to your feedback in further
editions of this Workbook.*

The Publisher

Contents

Super Senses

1. Fill in the blanks with appropriate words given in the box.

> *silkworm, criminals, hunters, sloths, langur, food, smell, mosquitoes, 4, 6, poachers*

(i)   As the ants move, they leave their __________ on the ground.

(ii)   __________ can find you by the smell of your body.

(iii)   Some birds like kites, eagles and vultures can see __________ times as far as we can.

(iv)   __________ looks like a bear and sleeps for about 17 hours a day.

(v)   People who kill animals are called __________ and __________.

2. Write 'T' for True and 'F' for False statements.

(i)   Most of the birds can move their eyes.

(ii)   Animals can see more colours than humans can.

(iii)   Dogs know if another dog has come into their area by movement.

(iv)   Sloths live for about 20 years.

(v)   Animals that are awake at night can see things only in black and white.

(vi)   A tiger roar can be heard upto 6 km away.

3. Multiple Choice Questions (MCQs).

(i)   Which animals can see things only in black and white?

(a) Birds   (b) Bats

(c) Rats   (d) Snakes

(ii)   Which of the following animals does not warn other animals of danger?

(a) Birds   (b) Langurs

(c) Bats   (d) Dolphins

(iii) Which animals are not seen in winters?

    (a) Birds   ☐   (b) Langurs   ☐

    (c) Lizards   ☐   (d) All of them   ☐

(iv) Where is Jim Corbett National Park?

    (a) Delhi   ☐   (b) Jharkhand   ☐

    (c) Uttar Pradesh   ☐   (d) Uttarakhand   ☐

(v) Where is Ghana National Park?

    (a) Delhi   ☐   (b) Haryana   ☐

    (c) Rajasthan   ☐   (d) Uttarakhand   ☐

4. What senses do the following animals use to find their food.

Animals	Senses		Animals	Senses
(i) Dog	__________		(ii) Eagle	__________
(iii) Ant	__________		(iv) Tiger	__________
(v) Snake	__________		(vi) Mosquito	__________

5. Match the pictures of the animals on the right with their description on the left.

(i) It can find its female by her smell.   (a)

(ii) It turns its head to see around.   (b)

(iii) It can feel vibration on the ground.   (c)

(iv) It can make different sounds to give message to other animals.   (d)

(v) It sleeps in the cold season.   (e)

6. Many animals are killed and their parts are sold. Match the animals with the part for which they are killed.

	Animals		Part of their body
(i)	Elephant	(a)	Horns
(ii)	Rhinoceros	(b)	Skin
(iii)	Crocodile	(c)	Musk
(iv)	Deer	(d)	Tusk
(v)	Snake	(e)	Skin

7. Categorise the following things on the basis of their smell as 'Good' or 'Bad' and fill in the columns below.

garbage dump, flower, dirty socks, petrol, rotten food, fish, coffee, pickle, soap, raw egg

Good Smell	Bad Smell

8. Give reasons for the following behaviour of animals.

(i) As you walked past a sleeping dog, its ears shot up at once.

(ii) You were eating in the playground and an eagle suddenly flew down and took away your roti.

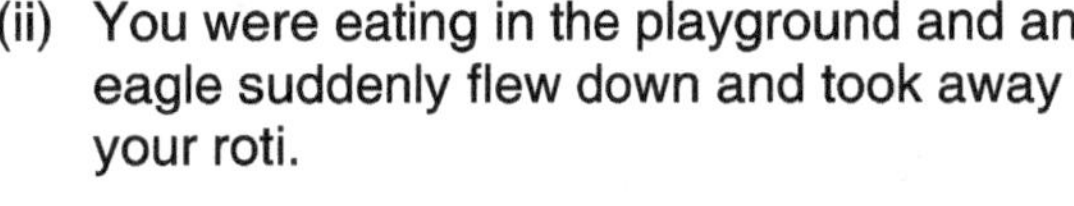

(iii) Dogs sniffing here and there on the road.

(iv) Sea animals suddenly behave in a different manner.

____

(v) Birds move their neck very often.

____

9. Names of some animals are given below. Make smiley (☺) in front of the animals that can see various colours and frowny (☹) in front of the animals that can see only black and white colours.

(i) Crow ◯

(ii) Bat ◯

(iii) Dog ◯

(iv) Cow ◯

(v) Fox ◯

(vi) Owl ◯

10. Write short notes on

(i) Differences in sleeping time of the animals.

____

(ii) Alarm calls given by different animals.

____

Short Answer Type Questions

11. Answer the following questions in brief.

(i) Why are lizards not seen in winters?

(ii) Why are dogs used in special search operations by police?

(iii) How can most of the birds see two different things at a time?

(iv) Why do snakes react to sounds although they do not have external ears?

(v) How did the tribes living in Andaman Islands managed to save themselves from the tsunami?

12. Observe the picture and answer the following questions.

(i) What is the name of the animal seen in the picture?

(ii) How does this animal warn other animals of its area about the danger?

Long Answer Type Questions

13. The tiger is one of the most alert and strong animal and yet today tigers are in danger. Answer the following questions about tiger.

   (i) Which sense of the tiger is very strong? How does this sense help the animal in finding food?

   (ii) How does a tiger mark its area?

   (iii) What helps a tiger to move in the dark?

   (iv) Tigers are endangered animals. How?

   (v) What steps are taken by the government to protect tigers?

14. Answer the following questions about sloths.

   (i) What do sloths eat?

   (ii) When do they move to another tree?

   (iii) Why do sloths come down from the tree once a week?

15. Answer the following questions about ants.

   (i) How do ants arrive soon after some sugar, jaggery etc is dropped on the ground?

   (ii) Where do the ants live?

   (iii) How are ants able to recognise their friends or group members?

Chapter 2

A Snake Charmer's Story

1. Fill in the blanks with appropriate words given in the box.

> *fertiliser, madaries, kalbeliyas, been, fangs, mark, death, medicines*

(i) ________ are the people who make the snakes dance by playing the ________ .

(ii) Snake charmers make ________ from the plants collected from the forests.

(iii) From the ________ of the bite *Saperas* could find out which snake has bitten the person.

(iv) Snakebite can even cause ________ on the spot.

(v) Poisonous teeth of the snakes are known as ________ .

2. Write 'T' for True and 'F' for False statements.

(i) *Saperas* used to play the *been* to entertain people.

(ii) Snake charmers know how to remove the poisonous teeth (fangs) of the snakes.

(iii) Snake charmers or Kalbeliyas used to gift snakes to their daughter when they got married.

(iv) All snakes are poisonous.

(v) The medicine for snakebite is available in all government hospitals.

3. Multiple Choice Questions (MCQs).

(i) Which of the following musical instruments are used in a *been* party?

(a) Tumba   (b) Khanjiri

(c) Dhol   (d) All of these

(ii) Khanjiri is made from dried

(a) Bottle gourd   (b) Bitter gourd

(c) Snake gourd   (d) Ridge gourd

(iii) *Kalbelia* is a kind of

    (a) dance form   (b) musical instrument

    (c) design   (d) song

(iv) The *saperas* carried snakes in

    (a) tin boxes   (b) bamboo baskets

    (c) cloth bags   (d) None of these

(v) What is the other name of the *Duboiya* snake?

    (a) Saw scaled Viper   (b) Sabre-toothed Viper

    (c) Russel's Viper   (d) None of these

4. Names of some snakes are given in jumbled form. Unscramble them and write their names in the space provided.

(i)   BACOR

(ii)   BUOYIDA

(iii)   TRAKI

(iv)   IFAA

How many of them are poisonous?

____

5. Give reasons.

(i) Snakes are friend of farmers.

____

(ii) Government made laws that no one can catch & keep wild animals.

____

Short Answer Type Questions

6. Answer the following questions.

(i) Why are snakes a treasure for the *saperas*?

(ii) How were *saperas* of great help to village people?

(iii) How does the poison of a snake enter a person's body?

(iv) The government has made a law that no one can catch and keep snakes. Why do you think this law is made?

(v) How has the law affected the snake charmer community?

(vi) How can snake charmers earn a living by the gift of playing the *been*?

(vii) Do the snake charmers treat the snakes badly? Explain your answer.

7. Observe the given picture and answer the following questions.

(i) Which musical instrument is shown in the picture?

(ii) The musical instrument is made up of which material?

(iii) Name the people who play such instrument.

(iv) What else do they carry to help people?

8. Observe the given picture and answer the following questions.

   (i) Name the dance form shown in the picture.

   (ii) What are the people who perform this dance form called?

   (iii) How is this dance associated with snakes?

9. Is there a medicine for snake bite? How is it made?

10. What are 'Naag Gumphan'? What are their uses?

11. In what ways can snake charmers share their knowledge about snakes?

Think, Find and Write

12. Like snake charmers, there are many communities who use animals for their livelihood.

   (i) Match the animal with the purpose they are used for.

Animals	Uses
(i) Cow	(a) carries load
(ii) Horse	(b) gives us eggs
(iii) Hen	(c) gives us wool
(iv) Sheep	(d) source of food
(v) Fish	(e) gives us milk

   (ii) Match the professions with the animals used in them.

Professions	Animals Used
(i) Snake charmer	(a) Elephants, Lions
(ii) Madaries	(b) Parrots
(iii) Fortune teller	(c) Snakes
(iv) Circus people	(d) Monkeys

Chapter 3

From Tasting to Digesting

1. Tick the food items that

(i) taste salty	Eggs ☐	Cooked vegetables ☐	Fish ☐	Raw vegetables ☐
(ii) taste sweet	Curds ☐	Tomatoes ☐	Jaggery ☐	Milk ☐
(iii) taste sour	Bread ☐	Tarmarind ☐	Cashew ☐	Sugar ☐
(iv) taste bitter	Potato ☐	Herbs ☐	Bitter gourd ☐	Amla ☐

2. Fill in the blanks with appropriate words given in the box.

> *salt, sugar, jaggery, lime, junk food, proper food, chew, gulp, glucose, Beaumont, Martin*

(i) We should eat food slowly and ____________ it well.

(ii) One should be given a ____________ and ____________ solution when one has loose motion and vomiting.

(iii) A ____________ drip is given to a patient for instant energy.

(iv) Dr ____________ found that food is digested in the stomach by an acidic juice.

(v) The food that is needed for proper growth and development of a child is called ____________ .

3. Give reasons.

(i) Sometimes people hold their nose before taking a medicine.

____

(ii) We cannot taste food properly when we have a cold.

____

Very Short Answer Type Questions

4. Answer in one word or one sentence.

(i) Name the process of breaking down food in simple form in our body.

(ii) Name the liquid in the mouth that helps in digestion.

(iii) Name the muscular bag in our body that churns food.

(iv) What term is used for the food items like burger and pizza that makes a person unhealthy?

Short Answer Type Questions

5. Observe the picture and answer the following questions.

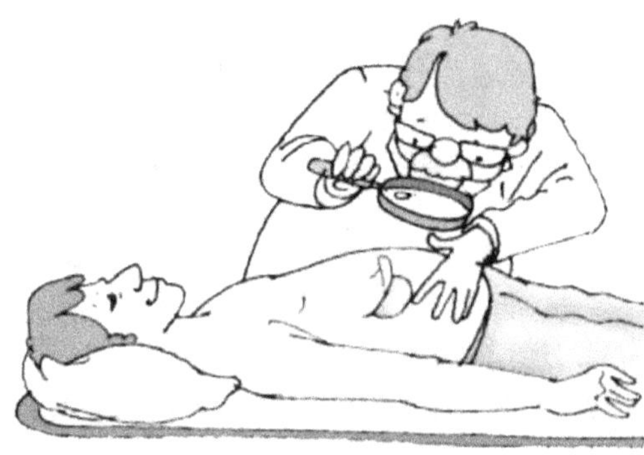

(i) Dr Beaumont did an experiment on digestion of food. What did he find in his experiment?

(ii) How is the digestion of food affected if a person is sad or not well?

6. How does our stomach help in the digestion of food?

7. What do you mean by proper food?

8. Observe the picture and answer the following questions.

   (i) What is being given to the patient in the picture?

   (ii) When and why is it given to the patient?

Think, Find and Write

9. Look at the three groups of food and answer the following questions.

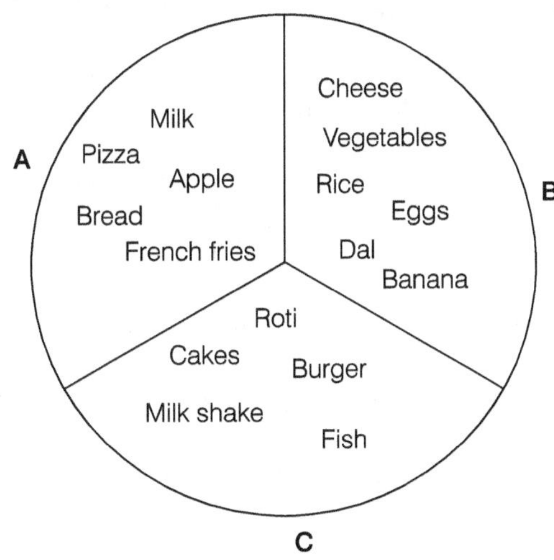

   (i) Which group has a healthy combination of food items?

   (ii) Which group will you choose and why?

   (iii) Among the group chosen by you, which food item to you dislike?

10. What happens when one eats the following?

   (a) Improper food

   (b) Insufficient food

11. How can you say that digestion begins in the mouth?

Chapter 4

Mangoes Round the Year

1. Fill in the blanks with appropriate words given in the box.

> *dust, muslin, green coriander, cooked rice, onion, drying, sweetening and salting, milk, sprouts, mangoes, ripe, unripe, sugar, fridge/refrigerator*

(i) _____________ can be kept fresh by boiling it.

(ii) _____________ can be kept fresh by keeping it in a dry open place.

(iii) *Mamidi tandra* is prepared from _____________ mangoes.

(iv) Pulp can be strained using _____________ cloth to remove the fibres.

(v) Fruits and vegetables in the home can be preserved by keeping them in the _____________ .

(vi) Making jam is a way of preserving the fruits by adding _____________ .

2. Multiple Choice Questions (MCQs).

(i) In which season does the food get spoiled easily?

(a) Winter   (b) Monsoon

(c) Summer   (d) Spring

(ii) What appears on moist bread when it is kept for a few days?

(a) Bacteria   (b) Fungus

(c) Virus   (d) Algae

(iii) Which of the following can be kept fresh by putting it in a bowl which is kept in a container with some water?

(a) Milk   (b) Cooked rice

(c) Green coriander   (d) Mangoes

(iv) Which of the following can be kept fresh by wrapping it in a damp cloth?

    (a) Cooked rice   (b) Green coriander

    (c) Onion, garlic   (d) All of these

(v) How many weeks does it take to prepare *Mamidi tandra*?

    (a) 2   (b) 4

    (c) 6   (d) 8

Very Short Answer Type Questions

3. Food can be preserved by several methods given below. Give one example of each that can be preserved in the following ways.

(i) Drying _____________   (ii) Freezing __________

(iii) Boiling _____________   (iv) By adding preservatives __________

(v) Sweetening and salting __________

4. What is the other name of *Mamidi tandra*?

____

Short Answer Type Questions

5. Answer the following questions briefly.

(i) How do we know that food has got spoiled?

____

(ii) What happens if a person eats spoiled food?

____

(iii) Why are glass jars and bottles dried well in the sun before filling them with pickles?

____

(iv) What do you mean by preservation of food?

____

6. Answer the following questions based on *Mamidi tandra*.

(i) How is *Mamidi tandra* prepared?

____

(ii) Why is a mixture of jaggery and pulp dried in the Sun?

____

(iii) Why was the mixture of jaggery and pulp covered with a clean saree?

____

7. Answer the following questions.

(i) What food items do you preserve in a refrigerator?

____

(ii) Make a list of food items that you keep in the freezer.

____

(iii) Name some items in which preservatives are added to make them last long.

____

Think, Find and Write

8. Suppose your family is going to your *nani's* house which is a 3 day journey. From the box below make a list of the food items that you will consume on the 1st, 2nd and 3rd day of the journey.

Puri	*Biscuits*	*Chips*	*Bananas*	*Chocolates*	*Apple*	*Fruit Juice*
Cheese	*Bread Butter*	*Potato Sabji*	*Fruit cake*	*Nuts*	*Pickle*	*Aam Papad*

(Hint: foods that spoil quickly should be consumed first)

1st day ____

2nd day ____

3rd day ____

9. Why is it important to read the date of expiry of a food item before buying it?

____

____

10. The mango garden of Chittibabu and Chinnababu was full of fruits in the summer holidays. This means that mangoes grow in the summer season. Write the names of some

(i) Summer fruits ____________________   (ii) Winter fruits ____________________

(iii) Fruits that grow throughout the year ____________________

Chapter 5

Seeds and Seeds

1. **Fill in the blanks with appropriate words given in the box.**

> air, water, warmth, space, light, cooling, heating, George Mestral, bursting, spoiled,
> sprouted, wet, pods, seeds, fruits, Europe, South America

   (i) Eating ___________ seeds is good for health.

  (ii) Seeds require ___________ , ___________ and ___________ to sprout.

 (iii) Velcro was discovered by ___________ .

 (iv) Soyabean seeds are scattered by ___________ of their ___________ .

  (v) Peas came from ___________ .

2. **Write 'T' for True and 'F' for False statements.**

   (i) Seeds are of different shapes, sizes, colours and textures.

  (ii) Some plants may grow without seeds.

 (iii) Dispersal of seed is essential so that the baby plant gets enough space, air and light.

 (iv) Tomatoes and green chillies came from South America.

3. **Multiple Choice Questions (MCQs).**

   (i) Which of the following is not a seed?

     (a) Chana   (b) Rajma

     (c) Arhar dal   (d) Lemon

  (ii) Which of the following is not necessary for a seed to grow?

     (a) Fertiliser   (b) Air

     (c) Water   (d) Warmth

(iii) Which of the following is not an agent of dispersal?

    (a) Animals   ☐   (b) Plants   ☐

    (c) Water   ☐   (d) Wind   ☐

(iv) Seeds of coconut plant are dispersed by

    (a) wind   ☐   (b) water   ☐

    (c) animals   ☐   (d) bursting   ☐

4. Give an example for each of the following categories.

  (i) Seeds used as spices.

 (ii) Seeds used as foodgrains.

(iii) Seeds used as pulses.

(iv) Seeds which scatter by bursting of the pod.

 (v) Seeds that scatter by sticking on fur of animals.

(vi) Seeds that scatter by wind.

(vii) Seeds that scatter by water.

5. Classify the plants according to the place of their origin.

Spinach	Tomato	Pea	Cabbage	Potato
Methi	Coffee	Green Chillies	Radish	Lady Finger

India	Europe	Africa	South America

Short Answer Type Questions

6. Give reason for the following.

 (i) Doctors sometimes advise sick people to eat sprouts.

(ii) Seeds kept in refrigerator do not sprout.

7. Answer the following questions.

    (i) What are the conditions a seed needs to sprout?

    (ii) What do you understand by dispersal of seeds? Why is it important?

    (iii) How was velcro discovered?

    (iv) State a few conditions that a seed needs to germinate.

8. Observe the following picture and answer the questions that follows.

    (i) What is the name of the plant given in the picture?

    (ii) Where is it found?

    (iii) How does the plant trap insects?

Think, Find and Write

9. Five types of seeds are given in Column A. There dispersal methods are given in column B. Match the columns.

Column A	Column B
(i) Seeds are heavy	(a) Animals eat the fruits and throw away the seeds
(ii) Seeds are small in size	(b) Some seeds are carried away by water
(iii) Seeds are travelling long distances	(c) Fruits/seeds get stuck to animal skins or clothes of humans
(iv) Seeds have hooks on them	(d) Plants burst open the pods for seeds to spread
(v) Seeds are light	(e) Seeds are blown by the wind

10. Seeds are kept in four different boxes under the conditions as given below.

Box A

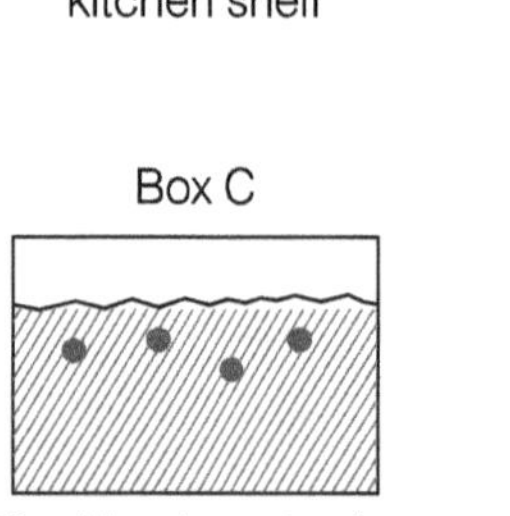

Soaking in water in
kitchen shelf

Box B

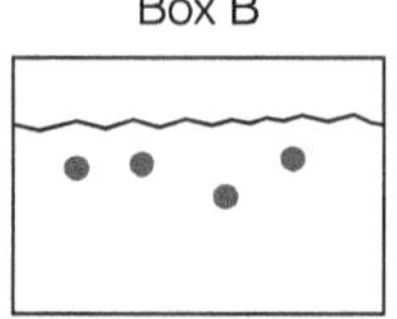

Keeping dry in
kitchen shelf

Box C

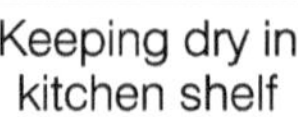

Soaking in water in
refrigerator

Box D

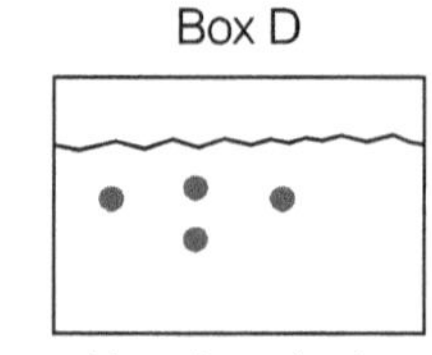

Keeping dry in
refrigerator

(i) In which of the above will the seeds grow quickest?

(ii) In which of the above will the seeds not grow at all?

Chapter 6

Every Drop Counts

1. Fill in the blanks with appropriate words from the box.

> *lake, necessity, precious, pond, stepwells, dharas, collect water, celebrate, rain*

(i) *Sar* means ___________ .

(ii) People in earlier times use to make ___________ for the travellers.

(iii) At some places, whenever lakes get filled up with rainwater the people gather around the lakes to ___________ .

(iv) Water is a ___________ of our life and should be used wisely.

(v) ___________ is the purest source of natural water.

2. Write 'T' for True and 'F' for False Statements.

(i) In earlier times people use to collect water in copper and brass pots.

(ii) The soil around trees should be covered with concrete and cement.

(iii) To overcome the problem of water shortage, directly put a pump in the Jal Board pipeline.

(iv) Water is pumped up from under the ground with the help of electric motors and bore-wells.

(v) Rise in population also causes water shortage.

3. Multiple Choice Questions (MCQs).

(i) How many interconnected lakes were there in *Ghadsisar*?

(a) 3　　　　(b) 5

(c) 7　　　　(d) 9

(ii) Al-Biruni came from

(a) Pakistan　　　　(b) Afghanistan

(c) Uzbekistan　　　　(d) Kazakhstan

(iii) Raised platforms made around lakes were also known as

    (a) *bavdis*   ☐   (b) *chabutras*   ☐

    (c) *naulas*   ☐   (d) *johads*   ☐

(iv) Which of the following arrangements was made for travellers?

    (a) Stepwell   ☐   (b) *Piau*   ☐

    (c) *Mashak*   ☐   (d) All of these   ☐

(v) *Bavdi* is another name of

    (a) pond   ☐   (b) lake   ☐

    (c) stepwell   ☐   (d) well   ☐

Very Short Answer Type Questions

4. Answer in one sentence.

    (i) From where do you get water in your homes?

    (ii) What can you do to minimise your water bill?

    (iii) How is the water provided in colonies where there is no supply of water through pipeline?

Short Answer Type Questions

5. Answer the following questions in brief.

    (i) Why decorated verandhas, large halls and rooms were made around lakes?

    (ii) Who was Al-Biruni? What did he write about the skill of Indian people in making ponds?

    (iii) What are Johads?

    (iv) Why are wells dried up now?

6. Observe the picture and answer the following questions.

   (i) Identify which lake is shown in the figure. Who built it?

   ____

   (ii) What is unique about this lake?

   ____

   (iii) Who used to take care of the lake?

   ____

   (iv) Is the lake in use these days?

   ____

7. Observe the picture and answer the following questions.

   (i) Where can we find such houses?

   ____

   (ii) How is water saved with such a system in houses?

   ____

8. Observe the picture and answer the following questions.

(i) Identify what is shown in the picture.

____

(ii) Why are so many steps made?

____

(iii) How is it different from a well?

____

Long Answer Type Questions

9. Why the stepwell in Jodhpur was cleaned after so many years? Why is it forgotten again?

____

____

10. The women in Alwar district of Rajasthan faced a lot of problem of water. What was it? How it was solved?

____

____

11. Write a short note on customs related to water in Uttarakhand.

____

____

12. Many places in Rajasthan get very little rainfall, yet most of the villages did not have shortage of water. Why?

Think, Find and Write

13. With the help of your teachers and friends, complete the following questions.

   (i) Write names of any two

     Lakes _________ , _________   Rivers _________ , _________

     Seas _________ , _________   Oceans _________ , _________

   (ii) Which is the biggest ocean in the world?

   (iii) Which is the longest river in the world?

   (iv) Which is the biggest freshwater lake in the world?

   (v) Which ocean is named after our country?

   (vi) Which is the longest river in our country?

14. Write the ways in which

   (i) Water is wasted in our country.

   (ii) Water is useful.

   (iii) Water can be conserved.

[Chapter 7]

Experiment With Water

1. Fill in the blanks with appropriate words given in the box.

> *sea water, mud, salt, sugar, Arabian, Dead, sinks, float, honey, soap water, big machine*

   (i) A needle _____________ in water.

  (ii) _____________ Sea is the saltiest sea in the world.

 (iii) _____________ is thick and flows slower than water.

 (iv) British put tax on _____________ .

  (v) _____________ is used to make salt.

2. Write 'T' for True or 'F' for False statements.

   (i) A flat dough will float on oil whereas puffed puri sink in it.

  (ii) Soap and soapcase both float in water.

 (iii) All oceans and seas have salty water.

 (iv) A person cannot get drown in Dead Sea.

  (v) Things once dissolved in water cannot be separated again.

 (vi) Oil flows faster than water.

(vii) The amount of water will reduce after heating it for a long time.

3. Multiple Choice Questions (MCQs).

   (i) Which of the following sinks in water?

      (a) Pin   (b) Coin

      (c) Eraser   (d) All of these

  (ii) Which of the following gets dissolved in water?

      (a) Egg   (b) *Ghee*

      (c) Sand   (d) *Mishri*

(iii) While preparing tea, which of the following does not get completely dissolved in water?

    (a) Sugar   ☐   (b) Milk   ☐

    (c) Tea leaves   ☐   (d) None of these   ☐

(iv) Which of the following can be separated from water by straining with cloth?

    (a) Oil   ☐   (b) Salt   ☐

    (c) Chalk powder   ☐   (d) Lemon juice   ☐

(v) In which year did Gandhiji go on the Dandi March?

    (a) 1929   ☐   (b) 1930   ☐

    (c) 1931   ☐   (d) 1942   ☐

(vi) Gandhiji went on Dandi March Yatra from

    (a) Dandi seashore to Ahmedabad   ☐   (b) Ahmedabad to Dandi seashore   ☐

    (c) Hyderabad to Dandi seashore   ☐   (d) Dandi seashore to Hyderabad   ☐

4. What will happen

    (i) If we put a raw egg in a glass filled with ordinary water.

    (ii) If we put a raw egg in a glass filled with salty water.

    (iii) If we pour some water and oil into a jar.

    (iv) If we vigorously mix water and oil in a jar.

Short Answer Type Questions

5. Answer the following questions briefly.

    (i) Why a person will continue to float in the Dead Sea, even if he does not know swimming?

    (ii) Why do clothes dry faster on a sunny day than on a cloudy day?

(iii) Where does the water from clothes go when they are dried in Sun? Name this process.

(iv) Why did Mahatma Gandhi undertake the Dandi March?

6. Read the following information and answer the questions that follows.

Shumaila put two drops each of groundnut oil, sugar solution and water on a stainless steel plate. She tilted the plate and found that some of the drops slid down quickly while some lagged behind.

(i) Which drops slid down faster?

(ii) Which drops slid down slowest? Why?

Think, Find and Write

7. Write the objects given in the box in one of the two types given below the box.

> leaf, ice, aluminium foil, pencil, bottle cap, soap, nail, paper, feather, pebble, spoon, empty plastic bottle, bottle full of water

Objects that sink in water

Objects that float in water

8. How can you separate the following?

(i) Salt from water

(ii) Chalk powder from water

(iii) Tea leaves from water

(iv) Mud from water

9. Water is called a 'Universal Solvent' because it can dissolve many substances in it.

(i) Encircle the things given below which can dissolve in water.

Coffee powder	Flour	Ice
Pepper	Detergent	Black salt
Cotton	Disprin	Fruit juice
Honey	Butter	Mud

(ii) Name two factors that help the things above dissolve faster.

A Treat For Mosquitoes

1. Fill in the blanks with appropriate words given in the box.

> *Ronald Ross, Beaumont, algae, fungus, flu, dengue fever, malaria, chikungunya, catterpillars, Anopheles, larvae, flies*

   (i) Malaria is spread by female mosquitoes known as __________ .

  (ii) Mosquitoes spread diseases like __________ and __________ .

 (iii) The green growth around the stagnant water is made up of __________ .

 (iv) Apart from mosquitoes, __________ also spread many diseases.

  (v) Dr __________ found that mosquitoes spread malaria.

2. Write 'T' for True and 'F' for False statements.

    (i) Malaria is spread only by one kind of mosquito.

   (ii) Blood for testing malaria is taken from the place where a mosquito has bitten.

  (iii) Children suffering from anaemia do not grow well and their energy levels are low.

  (iv) In municipal corporation schools, health check-ups are done and health cards are made for children.

   (v) Mosquitoes breed in stagnant water.

  (vi) Mosquitoes lay eggs in water only.

 (vii) Fish eat the mosquito larvae present in water.

(viii) Flies also bite like mosquitoes.

  (ix) The word 'Malaria' means bad air.

3. Multiple Choice Questions (MCQs).

(i) How much blood is needed to test malaria?

(a) 2-3 drops   ☐   (b) Half a syringe   ☐

(c) Full syringe   ☐   (d) Blood is not required   ☐

(ii) From early times which tree bark was used to prepare medicine for malaria?

(a) Teak   ☐   (b) Kadamb   ☐

(c) Coral Tree   ☐   (d) Cinchona   ☐

(iii) How much blood is needed to test for Anaemia?

(a) 2-3 drops   ☐   (b) Half a syringe   ☐

(c) Full syringe   ☐   (d) Blood is not required   ☐

(iv) Anaemia is caused by the deficiency of

(a) Calcium   ☐   (b) Iron   ☐

(c) Vitamin A   ☐   (d) Vitamin D   ☐

(v) In which season is malaria more common?

(a) Summer   ☐   (b) Winter   ☐

(c) Spring   ☐   (d) Monsoon   ☐

(vi) Ronald Ross got the Nobel Prize for

(a) Physics   ☐   (b) Medicine   ☐

(c) Chemistry   ☐   (d) Literature   ☐

(vii) Ronald Ross got the Nobel Prize in the year

(a) 1900   ☐   (b) 1902   ☐

(c) 1903   ☐   (d) 1905   ☐

4. Circle the food items rich in iron.

Curd	*Cauliflower*	*Jaggery*	*Potato*
Amla	*Banana*	*Spinach*	*Curry leaves*
French beans	*Apple*	*Milk*	

5. Give the reason.

(i) It is advised not to eat cut or uncovered food items.

(ii) We should put kerosene oil in fountains, water cooler, etc (where there is stagnant water).

Short Answer Type Questions

6. Answer the following questions.

(i) What is Anaemia?

(ii) What kind of diet is suggested for a patient of Anaemia?

(iii) What is given in municipal schools to anaemic children?

7. Observe the given picture and answer the following questions.

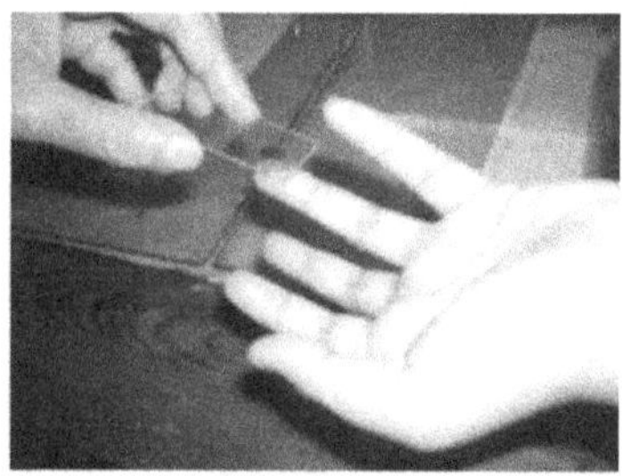

Pic. (a)

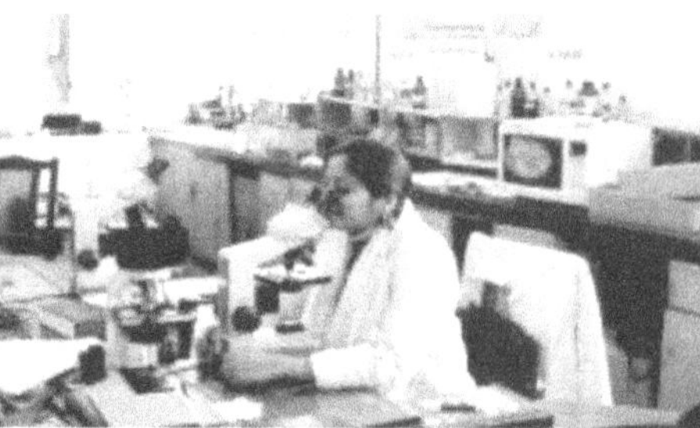

Pic. (b)

(i) Which test is being done in the pic. (a)?

(ii) Name the instrument that the doctor is using in pic. (b).

(iii) How can doctors find out that a person has malaria?

8. Look at Aarti's blood report and answer the following questions.

क्लीनिकल विकृति रिपोर्ट
CLINICAL PATHOLOGY REPORT
केंद्रीय सरकार स्वास्थ्य योजना
Central Govt. Health Scheme

20/06/2007

नाम/Name....**Aarti**.... आयु/Age..**12**.. स्त्री या पुरुष/Sex....**Female**....

रोग की पहचान/Diagnosis ....**Anaemia** (अनीमिया).........................

Normal Range
(नॉरमल रेंज)

Haemoglobin ....**8**.... gm/dl   12 to 16gm/dl
(हीमोग्लोबिन)

Pathologist

   (i) How old is Aarti and what is the minimum amount of haemoglobin required in her body?

   (ii) What do the blood report tell us about Aarti?

9. Observe the picture and answer the following questions.

   (i) Identify the great scientist in the picture.

   (ii) What contribution has he made in the field of science?

   (iii) Write a few lines about his research.

Long Answer Type Questions

10. List some activities in and around your house which you can perform to prevent the diseases like Malaria, Dengue and Chikunguniya.

11. What is larvae? What do they look like and how do they spread diseases?

12. Why people are advised to clear the stagnant water immediately?

Think, Find and Write

13. Look at the various preventive measures shown in the picture and write 2-3 lines on each. Also give some other preventive measures against mosquito bites.

14. Look in your surroundings and find out how flies cause diseases even though they do not bite us.

Chapter 9

Up You Go

1. Fill in the blanks with appropriate words given in the box.

> *blisters, bleeding, Mizo, Tamil, Telugu, skates, sticks, pegs, nails, hooks, women, children,*
> *45°, 90°, Bachhendri Pal, Sangeeta, tomatoes, cucumbers, 2nd, 5th, 8000, 8848*

  (i) Sangeeta had ___________ on her feet.

  (ii) Khondonbi spoke only ___________ language.

  (iii) The rope was tightly fixed to ___________ on both sides of the river.

  (iv) Body should be kept at an angle of ___________ while climbing a rock.

  (v) Khondonbi plucked two ___________ from the field.

  (vi) Mountaineers walk on snow with the help of ___________ .

  (vii) On the last day of camp, the 'Best Performance Award' was given to ___________.

  (viii) ___________ became the first Indian woman and the ___________ woman in the world to reach Mount Everest.

  (ix) The height of Mount Everest is ___________ metres.

2. Write 'T' for True and 'F' for False statements.

  (i) Sangeeta was a teacher from Kendriya Vidyalaya. ☐

  (ii) A group leader walks ahead of the group. ☐

  (iii) Medical check-ups were done every morning. ☐

  (iv) Tekla village is at height of 2600 m. ☐

  (v) Mountaineers make food on *chulhas*. ☐

  (vi) Mount Everest is called *Sagarmatha* in Nepal. ☐

3. Give reason for each of the following.

    (i) Sangeeta could not talk to Khondonbi even once.

    (ii) Mountaineers take Vitamin C, Iron tablets and hot chocolate milk with breakfast.

    (iii) Everyone was pushing each other to go first for crossing the river.

    (iv) Mountaineers first observe the rocks carefully before beginning to climb.

    (v) Mountaineers get into the sleeping bags for sleeping in high mountains.

Very Short Answer Type Questions

4. Answer the following questions based on Bachhendri Pal's life.

    (i) Where did Bachhendri Pal spend her childhood?

    (ii) Which institute did Bachhendri Pal join to learn mountaineering?

    (iii) Who was Bachhendri Pal's guide?

    (iv) Bachhendri Pal was selected to climb which mountain in 1984?

    (v) Define the terms (a) Sleeping bags   (b) Rock climbing

Short Answer Type Questions

5. Answer the following questions in brief.

   (i) What did Sangeeta Arora decide to do when she saw blisters on her feet on the second day of her camp? How did Brigadier Gyan Singh react to her problem?

   (ii) What do mountaineers use for their safety?

   (iii) What is rappeling?

   (iv) How did Sangeeta meet Bachhendri Pal?

   (v) What programme was there on last day of camp?

   (vi) Why did Bachhendri Pal put the Indian flag on the peak?

6. Answer the following questions based on the experience of Sangeeta Arora.

   (i) What was her group number?

   (ii) Who were the other members in her group?

   (iii) Who were other members in the camp?

   (iv) Who was the leader of her group?

   (v) In which institute was she learning mountaineering?

   (vi) Who was the director of their Adventure Course?

7. Observe the picture and answer the following questions.

   (i) What are the girls doing in the picture?

  (ii) Why were double layered plastic sheets used for the tent and the ground?

 (iii) In order to keep the insects and reptiles away, something is done around the tent. What is it?

Long Answer Type Questions

8. Answer the following questions in detail.

   (i) What are the responsibilities of a group leader in mountaineering?

  (ii) How were Sangeeta and Khondonbi left behind from their group? How did they meet their group again?

 (iii) How did Bachhendri Pal survive the snow storm and reach the peak of Mount Everest?

 (iv) Which incident transformed Sangeeta into a confident and courageous person?

9. Make a list of things that mountaineers keep in their rucksack.

(i) ____________   (ii) ____________   (iii) ____________   (iv) ____________

(v) ____________   (vi) ____________   (vii) ____________   (viii) ____________

(ix) ____________   (x) ____________   (xi) ____________   (xii) ____________

Think, Find and Write

10. Find out.

(i) The highest peak in the world, its height and located in which country.

____

(ii) The highest peak in India, its height and located in which state.

____

(iii) The first man to climb Mount Everest.

____

(iv) The names of two mountaineering institutions in India.

____

11. Your school is conducting an adventure camp where rock climbing and river crossing will be done. Make a list of things and safety equipments that you will carry. Also design a flag for your camp.

Chapter 10

Walls Tell Stories

1. Fill in the blanks with appropriate words given in the box.

> *Moti Darwaza, Fateh Darwaza, harmless, atomic, nuclear, clay, mud, Mughal, Aurangzeb, Qutubshahi, carvings, paintings*

(i) _________ Sultans lived in Golconda from 1518-1687.

(ii) Guns and cannons were used in the past. These days many countries have _________ bombs.

(iii) If a person stands at _________, whatever he speaks can be heard at the king's palace.

(iv) _________ pipes were used to carry water to different places in the palace.

(v) There were beautiful _________ on the walls of Golconda fort.

2. Write 'T' for True and 'F' for False for the following statements.

(i) In the year 1200 AD, the Golconda fort was made of bricks.

(ii) People like farmers and workers also lived in Golconda fort.

(iii) Golconda fort has four floors.

(iv) A long deep ditch (pit) was made along the Golconda fort walls.

(v) In the fort, a thousand years ago, tribal people were able to extract copper and tin from the mines.

3. Multiple Choice Questions (MCQs).

(i) How many bastions are there in Golconda fort?

(a) 67　　　　(b) 78

(c) 87　　　　(d) 92

(ii) Which emperor's cannon is kept in Golconda fort?

(a) Qutubshahi　　　　(b) Abul Hassan

(c) Aurangzeb　　　　(d) None of these

(iii) The gun placed in Golconda Fort was made of

    (a) copper ☐   (b) iron ☐

    (c) steel ☐   (d) bronze ☐

(iv) For how long did Aurangzeb army camp outside Golconda fort to capture it?

    (a) 2 weeks ☐   (b) 8 weeks ☐

    (c) 2 months ☐   (d) 8 months ☐

(v) Where is Golconda fort?

    (a) Ahmedabad ☐   (b) Hyderabad ☐

    (c) Udaipur ☐   (d) Jaipur ☐

4. Give reason.

(i) Bastions were even higher than the fort walls.

____

(ii) Aurangzeb's army could not get into the Golconda fort.

____

5. Using the clues given below, guess the word.

(i) The part of the wall that comes out in a round shape   _a_ _io_s

(ii) The big gun   _a_ _o_

(iii) The archs to move through   _e_ra_

(iv) A place where old items are kept   _u_eu_

(v) Leather bags to carry water   _a_ _a_

6. Circle the special features things of the Golconda Fort.

Swords	Jewellery	Sharp Iron Spokes
Factories	Huge gate	Roads
Carved walls	Thin walls	Burj
Big halls	Gardens	Fountains

Short Answer Type Questions

7. Answer the following in brief.

(i) How did the emperors and kings in earlier times make smaller kingdoms a part of their own kingdom?

(ii) What are bastions? Why holes were made in the bastions?

(iii) How was the water lifted to big tanks and fountains on the roof?

(iv) What were the arrangements of light and air in Golconda fort?

(v) Which things were found when the place around Golconda was dug?

8. Observe the figure and answer the following questions.

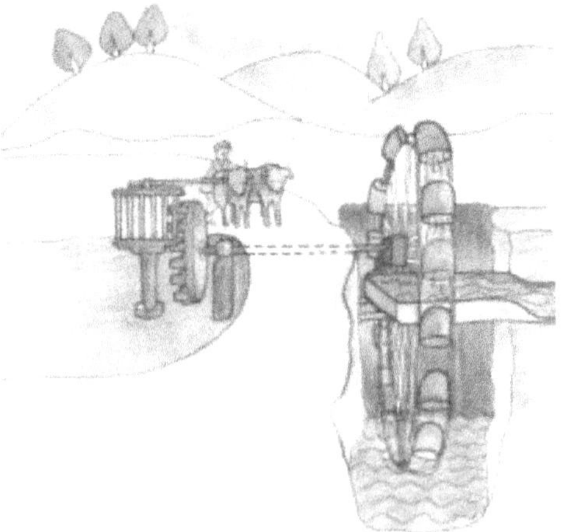

(i) Which animal is used to move the 'toothed wheel'?

(ii) In which direction would the 'toothed wheel' move?

(iii) How was water lifted from the well?

9. Look at map and complete the story.

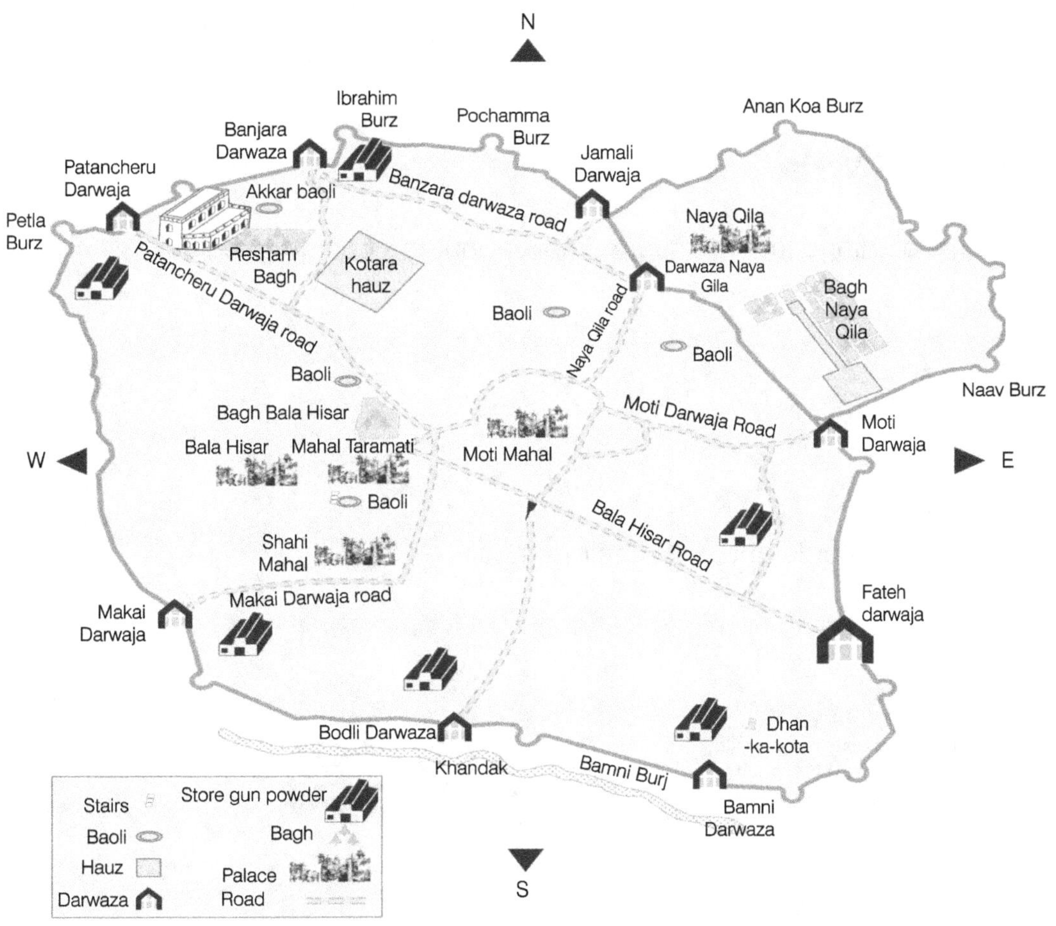

I always wanted to visit Golconda Fort. I entered the fort through Bodli Darwaza and headed __________ (north/south) towards Moti Mahal which is in the __________ (centre/corner) of the fort. From there Bagh Naya Qila is in __________ (west/east) while Bala Hisar is in __________ (east/west). To see Naya Qila, I should go __________ (south/north) and to see Dhan-ka-kota I must go __________ (west/south) from Moti Mahal. But I decided to see Resham Bagh which is __________ (east/west) of Katora Hauz. I visited all the places and finally exited from Banjara Darwaza.

Long Answer Type Questions

10. Answer the following in 40-50 words.

(i) Describe about the intelligent architecture of the Golconda fort.

(ii) 'It is important to have museum'. Give reason.

____

____

Think, Find and Write

11. Write names of things that help us to know about the past [e.g. coins]

(i) _______________   (ii) _______________

(iii) _______________   (iv) _______________

(v) _______________   (vi) _______________

12. Identify the monuments and write their names.

_______________   _______________   _______________

_______________   _______________   _______________

Chapter 11

Sunita in Space

1. Fill in the blanks with appropriate words given in the box.

> *seas and oceans, land, Kalpana's, her, 9 months, 6 months, seas, clouds, blobs, bubble*

(i) The blue parts of the globe are ___________ .

(ii) Water floats like ___________ in space.

(iii) Sunita Williams has spent more than ___________ in space.

(iv) Sunita Williams could only make out the ___________ and the ___________ on the earth from space.

2. Write 'T' for True or 'F' for False statements.

(i) The sky, stars, sun and moon are inside the globe.

(ii) Food and water also float in a spaceship.

(iii) The earth pulls everything towards itself.

(iv) Sunita Williams went 630 km away from the earth.

(v) There are lines drawn on the ground between the states and countries.

3. Multiple Choice Questions (MCQs).

(i) Which of the following countries is situated on the lower part of the globe?

(a) England   (b) Brazil

(c) Germany   (d) USA

(ii) Which of the following are in space?

(a) Stars   (b) Moon

(c) Sun   (d) All of these

(iii) Which of the following festivals is related to the moon?

(a) Gurupurab   (b) Dushhera

(c) Eid   (d) Christmas

(iv) In high school, Sunita wanted to become a

    (a) teacher   ☐   (b) helicopter pilot   ☐

    (c) diver   ☐   (d) astronaut   ☐

(v) When did Sunita Williams set a new record for the longest space flight by a woman?

    (a) In 2002   ☐   (b) In 2005   ☐

    (c) In 2007   ☐   (d) In 2009   ☐

4. Observe the following pictures and write their numbers against the correct statements associated with them.

①   ②   ③

④   ⑤

Statements

(i) Look my hair is standing, no problem while working.   ☐

(ii) Sunita outside the spaceship, really in space.   ☐

(iii) We take off.   ☐

(iv) Where is this food flying away?   ☐

(v) Our feet don't stay on the floor.   ☐

5. Give reason.

(i) People living in Brazil and Argentina (countries on the lower part of the globe) do not fall off.

(ii) The sea water doesn't fall off.

(iii) Paper has to be stuck to the wall of a spaceship in space.

(iv) In space there was no need to use a comb.

(v) In a spaceship, space travellers did not experience the pull of the earth.

(vi) When we throw a ball in the air it falls back.

(vii) Children always slide down the slide and not slide up.

(viii) From mountains, water flows downwards, not upwards.

6. Write if the following incident will take place in space or on the earth in the table below.

(i) Person floats in air

(ii) Water stays in a bucket

(iii) Water takes shape of blobs

(iv) Food floats

(v) Hair keeps standing

(vi) Water falls downwards on a slope

(vii) A coin comes back to our hand when thrown up

Earth	Space

7. Answer the following in one word or one line.

(i) From whom was Sunita inspired in her childhood?

(ii) What did Sunita want to become when she was young?

(iii) What did she become when she grew up?

(iv) What record did Sunita make?

(v) Why did Sunita want to become a school teacher?

Short Answer Type Questions

8. Answer the following questions briefly.

(i) Who is Sunita Williams? Why did she come to India?

(ii) What was Kalpana's dream?

(iii) How did Sunita describe her view of the earth from space?

(iv) A coin and a small piece of paper (size equal to the coin) are dropped from the same height and at same time. The coin reaches the ground first. Why?

(v) 'All the lines on the maps are made by us, they are in our minds'.

(a) Who said these words?

(b) What do you understand from these words?

Long Answer Type Questions

9. How does the earth appear from the surface of the moon?

10. Sunita Williams explained that they (space travellers) do very simple things differently like:

(i) sitting at one place

(ii) washing their face

(iii) eating food

(iv) combing

How do they do these? Why?

Think, Find and Write

11. Observe the given shapes of the moon

Find out

(i) Put a tick mark on the shape when it will be full moon.

(ii) Put a tick mark on the crescant moon.

(iii) Put a tick mark on no moon night.

12. Explain the terms given below

(i) Astrology

(ii) Shooting star

(iii) Spaceship

(iv) Satellite

(v) Globe

13. Identify the following space travellers and write few lines on each.

____

____

____

____

____

____

____

____

____

____

____

____

14. Complete the crossword with the help of the clues given.

Across

1. A meteorite which catches fire when it enters the earth's atmosphere.

3. The sky, stars, sun and moon are all in ________________ .

7. The moon when it appears perfectly round in the sky.

Down

2. A vehicle designed to travel in space

4. Our planet

5. Organisation for which Sunita Williams works

6. It is used for the TV, telephones and weather reports

8. Model of the earth

Chapter 12

What if it Finishes?

1. Fill in the blanks with appropriate words given in the box.

> pipes, machines, borewells, driller, petrol pump, shop, cars, bicycle, switch on, switch off, Hyderabad, Ahmedabad, wet, damp

(i) Adalaj stepwell is about 18 km from ____________ .

(ii) Generally, we don't see any ____________ on highway.

(iii) Vehicles stop at a ____________ for fuel.

(iv) ____________ the engine when you stop the car at red light.

(v) Through ____________ and ____________ petroleum is pumped out of the earth.

(vi) There is lot of smoke when ____________ wood is burnt.

2. Write 'T' for True or 'F' for False statements.

(i) Vehicles on the road make noise.

(ii) The problem of traffic jams is due to increased number of vehicles.

(iii) It is not safe to go on speeding vehicles.

(iv) Rates of petrol are different in different cities.

(v) Oil can be found everywhere under the ground.

(vi) Oil is formed naturally and quickly.

(vii) Oil pumped out from the ground is a smelly, thick, dark coloured liquid.

(viii) Electricity can be used to run vehicles.

3. Multiple Choice Questions (MCQs).

(i) Which of the following fuels gives least smoke?

(a) Petrol   (b) CNG

(c) Diesel   (d) None of these

(ii) To clean oil found deep down in the earth, it is sent to

    (a) pumps   ☐   (b) oil depot   ☐

    (c) refinery   ☐   (d) mills   ☐

(iii) Which of the following is obtained from petroleum?

    (a) Wax   ☐   (b) LPG   ☐

    (c) Coal tar   ☐   (d) All of these   ☐

(iv) Which gas is used for cooking in homes?

    (a) CNG   ☐   (b) LPG   ☐

    (c) Both (a) and (b)   ☐   (d) None of these   ☐

(v) How many people in our country use *uple*, wood and dry twigs to cook food?

    (a) Half of the people   ☐   (b) One fourth of the people   ☐

    (c) Two thirds of the people   ☐   (d) All the people   ☐

4. Give reason.

(i) The majority of people in our country use *uple*, wood and dry twigs, etc as fuel.

____

(ii) CNG is a superior fuel to petrol.

____

Short Answer Type Questions

5. Answer the following questions briefly.

(i) What problems can we have from the following?

    (a) smoke coming out of vehicles.

____

    (b) noise of vehicles.

____

(ii) What did the child decide to discuss with his Baba about saving oil?

____

(iii) Why did Manju said, "I will invent a car that runs on sunlight"?

(iv) Why is it better if fewer vehicles run on road?

6. Read the following passage and answer the questions that follows.

Treasure From The Earth

It is not easy to find out where oil is, deep down below the earth. Scientists use special techniques and machines to find this out. Then through pipes and machines petroleum is pumped up. This oil is a smelly, thick, dark coloured liquid. It contains many things mixed in it. To clean and separate these, it is sent to a refinery. Have you heard of a 'refinery'?

It is from this 'petroleum' or oil that we get kerosene, diesel, petrol, engine oil and fuel for aircraft. Do you know that LPG (cooking gas), wax, coal tar and grease are also obtained from this?

It is also used in making several other things like plastics and paints.

(i) From where do we get petroleum?

(ii) How much time does it take for the formation of oil?

(iii) How is it extracted?

(iv) Can extracted oil be used in same form?

(v) Where is the oil (petroleum) sent after it is extracted? Why?

(vi) Name any five products obtained from oil (petroleum).

Long Answer Type Questions

7. What problems will we face in the future due to increasing number of vehicles? Suggest some ways to deal with the problems.

8. Observe the picture and answer the questions that follows.

(i) What is the lady carrying with her in the basket? Why?

____

____

(ii) Is it safe to use it? Why?

____

____

9. Look at the following bar charts and answer the questions that follows.

Change in fuel use over twenty years

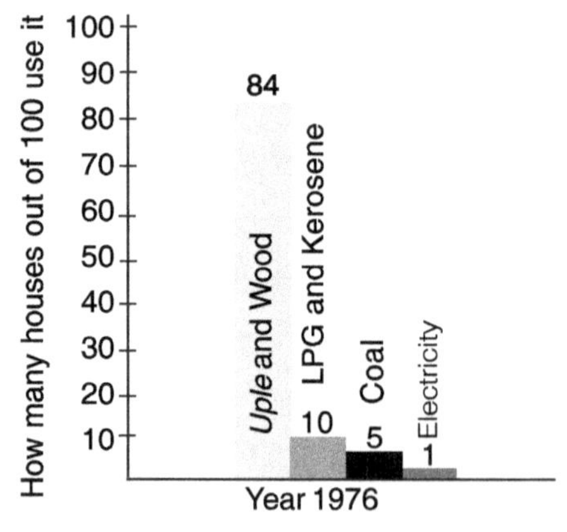

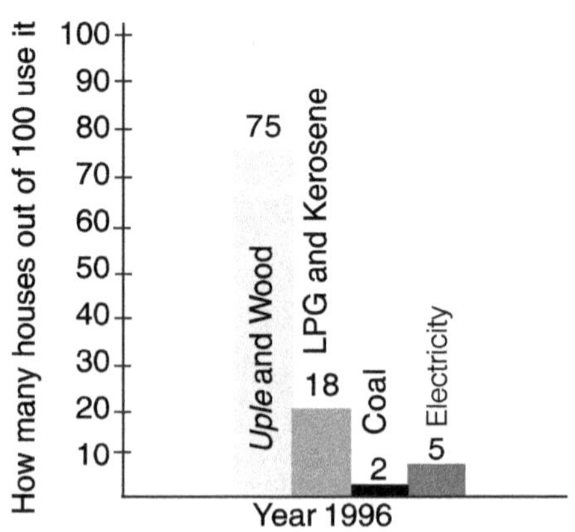

(i) In 1976 which fuel was used the

(a) maximum   (b) minimum

____

(ii) In 1996 which fuel was used the

(a) maximum   (b) minimum

____

(iii) In 1976, electricity was used in _________________ houses and in 1996 this increased to
_________________ . This means that in twenty years their use increased by _________________ %.

(iv) Consumption of which fuels has decreased from 1976 to 1996?

____

(v) Consumption of which fuels has increased from 1976 to 1996?

____

10. Look at the poster and answer the following questions.

(i) Do we have limited or unlimited reserves of fuel?

____

(ii) List any five ways in which you can save petrol.

(a) ____

(b) ____

(c) ____

(d) ____

(e) ____

Think, Find and Write

11. Put a (✓) on the vehicles which run without fuel and a (✗) on the vehicles which run using fuel.

(i) Train

(ii) Rickshaw

(iii) Aeroplane

(iv) Bicycle

(v) Autorickshaw

(vi) Horsecart

(vii) Ship

(viii) Bus

(ix) Scooter

(x) Car

12. In each use, write what may be used in its place if it finishes?

13. Journey of Petrol

The statements given below show how petrol reaches vehicles for use, but these are not in correct order. Put the numbers against each of these to make their sequence correct.

(i) Petrol reaches petrol depot

(ii) Petrol filling in the car

(iii) Petroleum oil dug out

(iv) Petrol transported to petrol pump

(v) Petroleum cleaned in refinery

(vi) Petroleum oil transported

14. Write

(i) The full form of

(a) CNG

(b) LPG

(ii) Any two oil refineries in India with their location.

(iii) Countries having large oil reserves.

A Shelter So High

1. Fill in the blanks with the appropriate words given in the box.

> *Shikara, houseboat, donga, Loner, Jumbo, Ladakh, welcome, bye, 50, 5, 80, 8, 1400, 2800, Mumbai, Jammu, dab, mehraab*

   (i) Gaurav Jani went on a long journey with his motorcycle named ____________ .

   (ii) The distance between Mumbai and Delhi is ____________ km.

  (iii) Delhi looked just like ____________ .

  (iv) In ____________ there were high snowcapped mountains and cold, flat ground.

   (v) Jule means ____________ .

  (vi) Tourists who come to Srinagar love to stay in a ____________ .

 (vii) Houseboats can be as long as ____________ feet and ____________ feet wide.

(viii) Many families in Srinagar live in a ____________ .

  (ix) ____________ are the beautiful arches in the old houses.

2. Write 'T' for True or 'F' for False statements.

   (i) Gaurav Jani's journey took about 4 months.

  (ii) The roads to reach Leh were difficult to travel on.

  (iii) Ladakh gets very little rainfall.

  (iv) Changthang is at height of almost 6000 m.

  (v) Changpa tribe has only 500 people.

  (vi) Changpas had horses and yaks.

 (vii) Changpas move from one place to another.

3. Multiple Choice Questions (MCQs).

   (i) Which of the following place is a 'cold desert'?

      (a) Manali   ☐   (b) Changthang   ☐

      (c) Ladakh   ☐   (d) Srinagar   ☐

  (ii) Where is Leh?

      (a) Changthang   ☐   (b) Ladakh   ☐

      (c) Srinagar   ☐   (d) Manali   ☐

 (iii) The carving on the ceiling of houseboat and big houses in Srinagar is called

      (a) motif   ☐   (b) panel   ☐

      (c) Khatamband   ☐   (d) Mehraab   ☐

  (iv) Some old houses in Srinagar have a special window which comes out of the wall known as

      (a) Lekha   ☐   (b) Donga   ☐

      (c) Dab   ☐   (d) Mehraab   ☐

  (v) Which of the following is not a type of house?

      (a) Dab   ☐   (b) Donga   ☐

      (c) Houseboat   ☐   (d) Rebo   ☐

  (vi) Bakarwal people live in houses made of

      (a) mud and lime   ☐   (b) stones and mud ☐

      (c) bamboos   ☐   (d) mud and hay   ☐

4. Give reason.

   (i) Roof is the most important part of the houses of Tashi.

____

  (ii) Goats are a treasure for the Changpa tribe people.

____

 (iii) Changpas graze their goats at higher and colder places.

____

  (iv) Each family puts a special mark on their animals.

____

(v) Houses on the mountain have a sloping roof.

(vi) Every lane in Kashmir has a bakery.

Short Answer Type Questions

5. Observe the picture and answer the following questions.

(i) Changpa people live in such tents. What do they call their tents?

(ii) Near the tents Changpas keep their animals. What do they call this place?

(iii) How are these tents made?

(iv) Why there is an opening in the tent?

6. Observe the figure and answer the questions that follow.

(i) Where are such houses found?

(ii) What are the special features of these houses?

____

(iii) For what purpose are the ground floors used in these houses?

____

7. Read the following passage and answer the questions that follow.

The World famous Pashmina Shawls

It is believed that a pashmina shawl is as warm as 6 sweaters! It is very thin yet very warm. The goats from which the soft pashmina wool is collected are found at very high altitudes of 5000 metres. In winter, temperature here drops below 0°C (down to −40° C). A coat of warm hair grows on the goat's body which protects it from extreme cold. The goats shed some of their hair in summer. This hair is so fine that six of these would be as thick as one hair of yours !

The fine hair cannot be woven on machines and so weavers of Kashmir make these shawls by hand. This is a long and difficult process. After almost 250 hours of weaving one plain pashmina shawl is made. Imagine how long it would take to make a shawl with embroidery.

(i) What is so special about pashmina shawls?

____

(ii) From which animal is the wool for pashmina shawl obtained? Where are these animals found?

____

(iii) What is the speciality of Pashmina wools?

____

(iv) Who makes these shawls? How?

____

8. Answer the following questions briefly.

(i) Why did Gaurav Jani go on such a long journey?

____

(ii) What all things did Gaurav Jani take with him on his journey?

____

(iii) Which lake and river are situated near Srinagar? What kind of houses are seen near the lake?

____

(iv) What things attract tourists to Srinagar?

(v) What is a *shikara*?

(vi) How was Gaurav feeling on his return journey?

Long Answer Type Questions

9. Write the similarities and differences in the life of Bakarwal people and the life of the Changpas.

Similarities

Differences

10. Gaurav was amazed to see the beautiful houses in Srinagar. He also made a photo album. What were the special features of these houses ? Explain in your own words.

Think, Find and Write

11. Answer the following

(i) What type of roofs are there in houses of Ladakh ?

(ii) What type of roofs are there in houses of Srinagar?

(iii) Why is there a difference between the roofs of houses in Srinagar and in Ladakh?

12. What were special features of houses in

Delhi	Leh	Changthang	Jammu

13. The names of types of house are given in jumbled form along with their pictures. Write their correct names in the spaces provided.

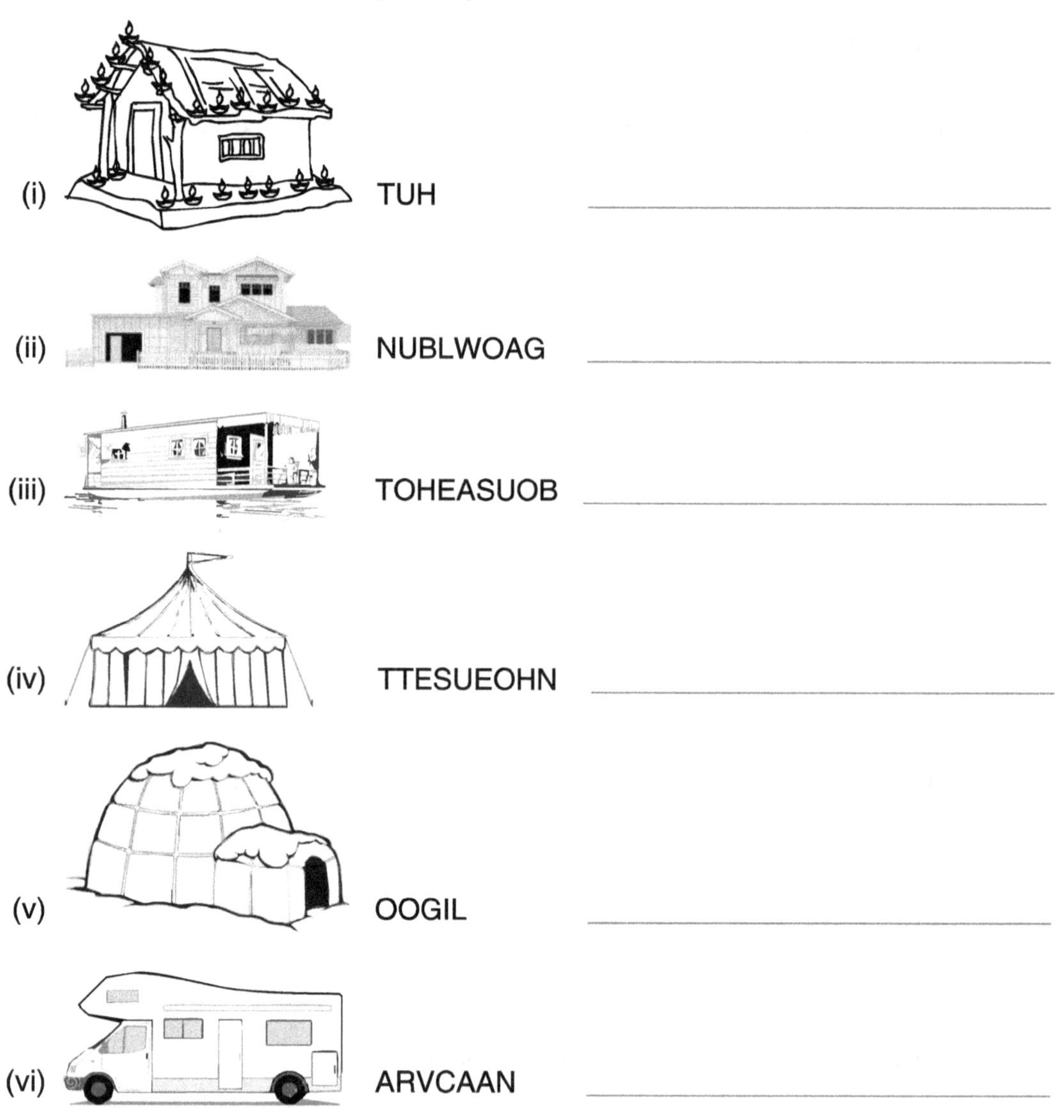

(i)   TUH   ________________________

(ii)   NUBLWOAG   ________________________

(iii)   TOHEASUOB   ________________________

(iv)   TTESUEOHN   ________________________

(v)   OOGIL   ________________________

(vi)   ARVCAAN   ________________________

14. Describe the different kinds of shelters in Ladakh and Kashmir which suit the needs of the local people.

____

____

Chapter 14

When the Earth Shook

1. Fill in the blanks with the appropriate words given in the box.

> *doctors, engineers, architects, scientists, army people, stand,*
> *lie down, 4, 6, 10, twisted, fractured, cold, fear, pain, grief*

(i) Jasma's leg got ___________ .

(ii) ___________ people of Jasma's village died.

(iii) ___________ and ___________ kept village people awake in the night.

(iv) ___________ tried to find out which areas have more chances of having an earthquake.

(v) ___________ and ___________ showed designs of houses which would not get damaged much in earthquake.

(vi) In case of earthquake ___________ under a strong thing and hold it.

2. Write 'T' for True or 'F' for False statements.

(i) Jasma was 15 years old when there was an earthquake in her city.

(ii) Jasma's village hospital was not much damaged.

(iii) Nobody was injured from Jasma's family.

(iv) Village women cooked food together at Motabapu's house and fed everyone.

(v) In case of an earthquake we should not go to an open area.

3. Multiple Choice Questions (MCQs).

(i) Which calamity occurred on 26th January, 2001?

    (a) Cyclone   (b) Flood

    (c) Earthquake   (d) Tsunami

(ii) When there is no rain, crops can fail; then there can be a

    (a) cyclone   (b) flood

    (c) famine   (d) drought

(iii) Excessive rainfall can lead to

    (a) tsunami   ☐   (b) flood   ☐

    (c) famine   ☐   (d) drought   ☐

(iv) Shortage of food and water can result in a

    (a) tsunami   ☐   (b) flood   ☐

    (c) famine   ☐   (d) drought   ☐

4. Read the TV report on Bhuj earthquake and answer the following questions.

At least a thousand people are feared dead in the earthquake that struck Gujarat this morning. Many thousands have been injured. Army jawans have been called in to help. At least a hundred and fifty buildings have fallen in the city of Ahmedabad. In these, there are a dozen multi-storeyed buildings. By this evening, around 250 bodies have been removed from these buildings. It is feared that several thousand people may still be trapped. Rescue efforts are on. There is perhaps no building in the city which has not developed cracks. The situation in Bhuj is even worse. People are running around in shock and panic. Within an hour of the earthquake the fire engines had reached and started work along with the local people. Offers to help are coming from all corners of the country and abroad.

(i) Where is Bhuj? When did the earthquake in Bhuj occur?

(ii) How many people died in the Bhuj earthquake? How many people got injured?

(iii) How many building got damaged in the Bhuj earthquake?

(iv) Why were people in panic?

(v) How the rescue operation was started in Bhuj?

5. Answer the following questions based on Jasma's bad experience of an earthquake.

(i) What is an earthquake?

(ii) When and where did the earthquake occur?

(iii) What was Jasma doing when the earthquake occurred?

(iv) How did the people of Kutch react?

(v) What damage was caused to the village and people there?

(vi) Did Jasma and her family members get injured?

(vii) Who was Motabapu? How did he help the other people of the village?

(viii) Who all came to help the village people? How did they help the village people?

(ix) Why were the people of the village afraid of making the houses again as the engineers were telling?

6. Observe the picture and answer the following questions.

(i) Which natural disaster is shown in the above picture? What should one do when this situation occurs?

(ii) How should people work to make their life normal again after a disaster?

7. How is the house shown in the picture below being made?

Think, Find and Write

8. Observe the picture and answer the questions that follow.

(i) Which natural calamity is shown in the picture?

(ii) Which areas in India are usually threatened by it?

(iii) Who gives warning to the people about natural calamities like these?

9. Observe the picture and answer the questions that follow.

(i) Which natural calamity is shown in the picture?

(ii) Which states in India are often affected by this calamity?

(iii) Who is providing relief to the people in such a calamity?

(iv) What kind of relief is being provided?

10. Help these people decide on the type of houses they should build in these places. Give reason.

(i) This place has high rainfall. The people want houses that can withstand heavy rain.

(ii) There have been many earthquakes in this place. People want houses that will be safe during earthquakes.

(iii) This place gets flooded very often. People want houses which will not be affected by floods.

11. How neighbours are helpful to us in a natural calamity? Give some qualities of a good neighbour.

12. With the help of the pictures given below fill the crossword.

2

5

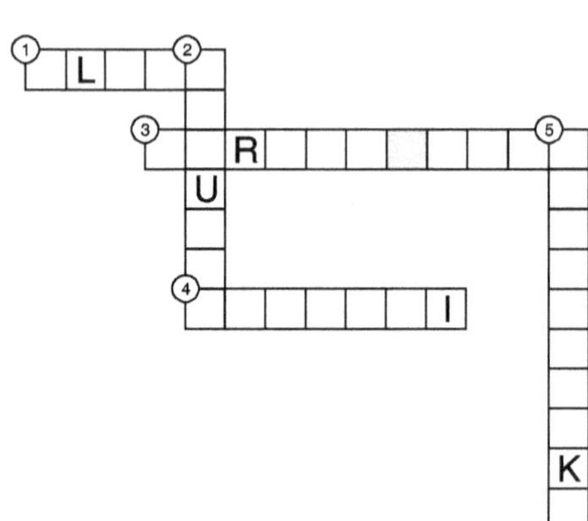

1

3

4

Chapter 15

Blow Hot, Blow Cold

1. Fill in the blanks with appropriate words given in the bracket ( ).

    (i) The air, we breathe out contains ___________ . (moisture/dust)

    (ii) When we blow air out of our mouth, our chest ___________, while when we breathe air in, our chest ___________ . (comes out/ goes in)

    (iii) ___________ air is light and rises. (Hot/Cool)

    (iv) ___________ air is heavy and comes down. (Hot/Cool)

2. Write 'T' for True or 'F' for False statements.

    (i) We blow on hot things to cool them and on cold things to warm them up.

    (ii) We blow on a burning fire to increase the supply of air to it.

    (iii) Our breath is cooler than hot tea and hence we blow on it to cool it.

    (iv) When you blow on a mirror in summers, you see drops of water on it.

    (v) Our heart beats slowly after we run, skip or exercise.

3. Mark (✓) for the actions in which blowing of air is used and (✗) for the cases in which blowing of air is not used.

    (i) Making bubbles from soap water   (ii) Skipping

    (iii) Sneezing   (iv) A woman fans her *chulha*

    (v) Eating food   (vi) Cooling tea

    (vii) While talking   (viii) Whistling

    (ix) While drinking water   (x) Playing the *flute*

Short Answer Type Questions

4. Answer the following questions from the woodcutter and Mian Balishtiye story.

   (i) Why did Mian Balishtiye hesitate before asking his first question from the woodcutter?

  (ii) Why was the woodcutter amazed to see Mian Balishtiye?

 (iii) Why did Mian Balishtiye begin to tremble with fear?

 (iv) How did the woodcutter make a *chulha* for boiling potatoes?

  (v) Why was the woodcutter blowing on the fire of his *chulha*?

5. Answer the following questions briefly.

   (i) How does your breath help to warm your cold hand in winters?

  (ii) Why does a popcorn seller fan the burning coal?

 (iii) How does your breath help to cool a cup of hot coffee?

 (iv) Why do people blow air on their spectacles before cleaning them?

6. Why is the girl blowing on the cloth?

7. What reasons did the woodcutter give to Mian Balishtiye for the following activities?

(a) Blowing on his hands.

(b) Blowing on the potatoes.

Think, Find and Write

8. Circle the musical instruments which are played by blowing air through them.

Guitar	Been	Harmonium	Piano	Flute
Whistle		Mridang		Mouth organ
Trumpet		Dholak		

Names of some other musical instruments played by blowing air through them.

______________________   ______________________

______________________   ______________________

9. This is a stethoscope.

   It is used by _______________________

   For what purpose is it used?

   ____

10. Count and write the number of breaths in a minute

    (i) when you are sitting still.

        _________________________________ times

    (ii) when you climbed a few stairs up.

        _________________________________ times

    (iii) when you have just finished some exercise.

        _________________________________ times

11. (i) Do you observe any change in the rate of breathing in different activities? Tick (✓) your
        choice.   Yes   No

    (ii) In which activity are the number of breaths taken by you and your friend highest in Q10?
         Why?

    ____

Chapter 16

Who Will Do This Work?

1. Complete the following passage with the help of words given in the box.

> dirty, clean, benefit, untouchables, someone else, convinced,
> Gandhiji, cleaning, village people, lesson, skill, argue

Narayan knew that the people who usually did this work were thought to be ___________

. He asked, "What is the use if the ___________ do not change their thinking? They have

become used to ___________ doing this work for them."

Gandhiji replied "Why? Don't you think the people who clean also ___________ from it.

They also learn a ___________ . To learn something is like learning a new ___________ .

Even if it is a ___________ job."

Little Narayan was not ___________ . He again argued, "Those who make a place

___________ but do not ___________ it should also learn lessons." Gandhiji and Narayan

continued to ___________ about this. But when he grew up Narayan always followed the

path shown by ___________ .

2. Write 'T' for True or 'F' for False statements.

(i)   People of one community have to do cleaning work.

(ii) Even guests had to clean their toilets in Gandhiji's Ashram.

(iii) Gandhiji used to clean toilets in Wardha.

(iv) Gandhiji said that everyone should not do cleaning work.

(v)   Gandhiji fought against untouchability.

(vi) The Indian Constitution was prepared under the leadership of Baba Saheb
      Ambedkar.

Very Short Answer Type Questions

3. Answer in one word or one sentence.

(i) Why do people do different kinds of jobs?

(ii) Write any two jobs that people would not like to do.

(iii) 'Every person should do every kind of work'. Who said these words?

Short Answer Type Questions

4. Answer the following questions briefly.

(i) In olden times, did children have to do the same work as their fathers and grandfathers did? Is it the same nowadays?

(ii) Who are untouchables? Does untouchability still exist in India?

(iii) Why some people, despite being educated, still have to do cleaning jobs?

(iv) How are people (who normally do cleaning) treated if they deny to do cleaning work?

5. Answer the following questions based on Gandhiji's work against untouchability.

(i) What was the name of Gandhiji's Ashram at Ahmedabad?

(ii) Who was Narayan? What was his job in the Ashram?

(iii) Who did the cleaning work in Gandhiji's Ashram?

(iv) How was cleaning work done in those days?

(v) What incident took place in Wardha? How did Gandhiji and Narayan react to the incident? Describe in your own words.

6. Answer the following questions based on Bhim Rao Baba Saheb Ambedkar.

(i) What incident of untouchability took place with him in Goregaon when he was young?

(ii) What did he become famous for?

Think, Find and Write

7. Write a short note on 'Swachh Bharat Abhiyan'—a campaign initiated by our Prime Minister, Mr Narendra Modi.

8. What is 'equality among people'? Name a right made by Central Government for giving equality to all people.

Chapter 17

Across The Wall

1. Fill in the blanks with appropriate words given in the box.

> *weak, player, state, district, boys, girls, everyone, best, hard work, cooperation, competition, courage, regret, injured, unhealthy, speak*

   (i) With a lot of guts and courage the team has reached the semifinals of a ___________ level tournament.

   (ii) While playing a game, play as a ___________ ; never think you are a girl or a boy.

   (iii) Sir says, "Keep playing even if you get a little ___________".

   (iv) ___________ between the members is the strength of team.

   (v) If you have a wish or a dream, have courage to ___________ about it and give your ___________ to fulfil them.

   (vi) It is good for ___________ to play.

2. Write 'T' for True or 'F' for False statements.

   (i) NBA was the first girls team in Mumbai.

   (ii) Zarin's brother was happy to see Zarin playing basketball.

   (iii) Both boys and girls go back to their homes as soon as they finished playing.

   (iv) People later began to accept that girls can also play.

   (v) NBA girls also played against a boys' team.

   (vi) Girls from the NBA team have gone to many places to play games.

3. Multiple Choice Questions (MCQs).

   (i) What is a full form of NBA?

     (a) Nagpada Basketball Authority   (b) Nagpada Basketball Association

     (c) National Basketball Authority   (d) National Basketball Association

(ii) Whose father was trained by Bacchu Khan?

(a) Khushnoor ☐ (b) Afsana ☐

(c) Afreen ☐ (d) All of these ☐

(iii) Whose mother encouraged her to play?

(a) Khushnoor ☐ (b) Afsana ☐

(c) Afreen ☐ (d) None of these ☐

(iv) Whose mother works in the flats?

(a) Khushnoor ☐ (b) Afsana ☐

(c) Afreen ☐ (d) Both Afsana and Afreen ☐

(v) Who was the coach of the NBA team?

(a) Bacchu Khan ☐ (b) Mustafa Khan ☐

(c) Noor Khan ☐ (d) None of these ☐

4. Read the following passage and answer the questions that follows.

Coach Sir

The coach who made this team, Noor Khan told us, "This part of Mumbai is very crowded. This is the only playground in this area. This is our small 'Bacchu Khan playground'. A person named Mustafa Khan used to live in our area. Everyone was afraid of him. But children were very fond of him, so everyone started calling him Bacchu Khan. There was no ground there, it was just muddy land. Bacchu Khan used to train children to play. We were among those children.

It is because of Bacchu Khan's devotion and training that players from this area are able to compete with teams of other countries. Like Bacchu Khan, I have trained the children of this area. Today, our team has some who play at the international level. Some have even won the Arjuna Award.

In the last few years, we have also prepared a girls' team here. Our girls play for the Maharashtra State team. They practise well with good discipline. Our boys and girls come from different types of families. Some are from poor homes and some from richer. Some study in Urdu medium and some in English. But once they come here, they all make a team."

(i) Who was Bacchu Khan?

____

(ii) Why was the playground named 'Bacchu Khan playground'?

____

(iii) Who was Noor Khan? What were the achievements of his team?

(iv) How were the girls of Maharashtra state team different from each other? How were the girls united?

5. Name the sport that is being played by girls in the picture.

Short Answer Type Questions

6. Answer the following questions in brief.

(i) Why were girls not encouraged to play sports in earlier times? What were they expected to do?

(ii) Who was Afreen's father's coach? How did the coach help Afreen's father?

(iii) Why could Afreen's father not become a good player?

(iv) How were the NBA girls trained? What activities and exercises they have to do?

(v) How was the girls' spirit when they played against the boys' team?

(vi) What is 'team spirit'?

(vii) How was the girls' experience in Sholapur?

Long Answer Type Questions

7. What difficulties did these girls have to face to become a basketball player?

Khushnoor

Afreen

Afsana

Zarin

8. List some benefits of playing sports.

Think, Find and Write

9. Name some

Individual Sports	Team Sports

10. Name the following sportswomen. Also write the name of the sports with which they are associated.

Name ___________________   Sport ___________________

Name ___________________   Sport ___________________

Name ___________________   Sport ___________________

Name ___________________   Sport ___________________

Name ___________________   Sport ___________________

11. How many players are there in a team of

(i) Hockey? ___________________   (ii) Basketball? ___________________

(iii) Cricket? ___________________   (iv) Kabaddi? ___________________

12. Write the National game of

(i) India ___________________   (ii) America ___________________

(iii) China ___________________   (iv) Australia ___________________

13. How much is the title of the chapter 'Across the Wall' relevant? Why is it named so? What do you learn from the girls of NBA? How can such players be further motivated?

____

____

Chapter 18

No Place for Us

1. Fill in the blanks.

   (i)   Jatrya was born in _________ village.

   (ii) People of Sinduri called them (Jatrya's family) _________ .

   (iii) Jatryabhai moved from _________ to _________ and from there he moved to _________ .

   (iv) A big wall built across the river is called a _________ .

   (v)   The only dream of Jatryabhai was to send his children to _________ .

2. Write 'T' for True and 'F' for False statements.

   (i)   Jatryabhai had a family of distant relatives in Mumbai who helped them to settle there. ☐

   (ii) There was hills and jungles near Khedi village. ☐

   (iii) In Khedi, people did not fall sick often. ☐

   (iv) Jatryabhai had to shift from Sinduri to Khedi. ☐

   (v)   Jatrya's parents were so sad about leaving Khedi that they died. ☐

   (vi) Roofs made of tin keep houses cool in summers. ☐

   (vii) People of Sinduri were very friendly with Jatrya's family. ☐

3. Observe the given picture and answer the following questions based on Jatryabhai's life in Khedi Village.

(i) Since when was Jatrya's family living in Khedi village? Were they happy there?

(ii) What did people of the village have to do for their living?

(iii) How did Jatryabhai earn money in Khedi?

(iv) How would people get medicines in Khedi?

(v) What was the social life in Khedi?

4. Observe the given picture and answer the following questions based on Construction of a Dam in Khedi.

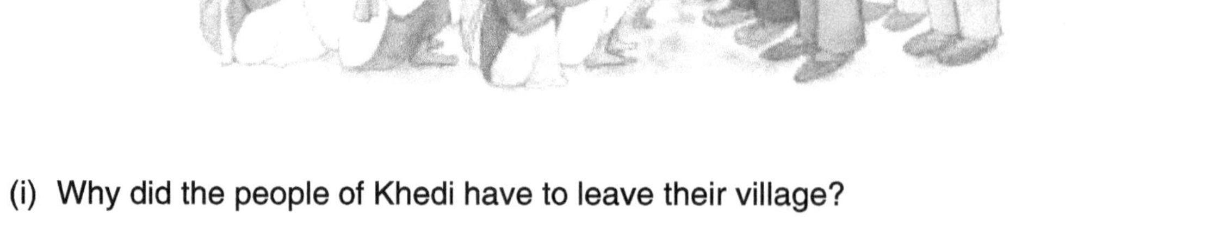

(i) Why did the people of Khedi have to leave their village?

(ii) Why did government officials and police come to Khedi village? How did children react on seeing the police?

(iii) What did government officials tell people of Khedi about the new village?

____

(iv) Did Jatrya want to shift from Khedi village? Why?

____

(v) Did Jatrya's parents want to shift from Khedi village? Why?

____

5. Observe the given picture and answer the following questions based on Jatryabhai's life in Sinduri.

(i) Why is Jatryabhai carrying an old tyre on his back?

____

(ii) Describe Jatrya's house in Sinduri.

____

(iii) How did Jatryabhai earn money in Sinduri? Was it sufficient?

____

(iv) How were the school and medical facilities in Sinduri?

____

(v) How was the social life in Sinduri? Where had the other people of Khedi village gone?

(vi) Was there electricity and enough water in Sinduri?

6. Jatrya was provided with a place in Sinduri village. Were the facilities sufficient? Give reasons for your answers.

7. Observe the given picture and answer the following questions based on Jatryabhai's life in Mumbai.

(i) For whom was Jatryabhai waiting?

(ii) What was the name of Jatryabhai's daughter? Why was she looking out of the window?

(iii) What did Jatryabhai do in Mumbai?

(iv) What kind of expenses did Jatryabhai's family have in Mumbai?

(v) What did young Sidya had to do to earn money? Does he go to school?

Think, Find and Write

8. Explain the following terms using the dictionary.

(i) Demolition

(ii) Transfer

(iii) Migration

(iv) Immigration

(v) Emigration

9. Name any five dams in India. Also mention their location and river on which they are made.

	Dams	Rivers
(i)		
(ii)		
(iii)		
(iv)		
(v)		

10. Building of dams, bridges, factories, etc are encouraged in the name of development and progress. But not all people benefit from this. How does building of dams affect the life of people who are displaced or asked to move from their place? Name the movement of our country which developed to resist the construction of big dams.

11. What are the differences between a city life and a village life?

Chapter 19

A Seed Tells a Farmer's Story

1. Fill in the blanks with appropriate words given in the box.

> *thresher, tractor, fresh, electricity, water threshers, charkha, bajra, maize*

(i) *Undhiya* was eaten with ___________ *rotis*.

(ii) As the people ate, they would remember how tasty the food was in the past ___________ from the field.

(iii) In earlier times, cotton was spun on the ___________ .

(iv) ___________ came due to the construction of a dam.

(v) The ___________ could do in a day what the bullocks would take many days to do.

2. Write 'T' for True or 'F' for False statements.

(i) Fertilisers from factories are cheaper than the natural fertilisers of earlier times. ☐

(ii) It is good for the soil to grow the same crop throughout the year. ☐

(iii) The quality of crop is better in modern times. ☐

(iv) Soil is not the same as it used to be. ☐

(v) Compost is a natural fertiliser. ☐

3. Multiple Choice Questions (MCQs).

(i) In older times good seeds were stored in dried

(a) brinjal ☐ (b) bitter gourd ☐

(c) gourd ☐ (d) cucumber ☐

(ii) Farmers in earlier times kept which leaves near seeds to protect them from insects?

(a) Mango ☐ (b) Banyan ☐

(c) Pine ☐ (d) Neem ☐

(iii) Which plant gives a signal that the top layer of the soil has become dry?

    (a) Unicorn   (b) Pitcher

    (c) Croton   (d) Lavender

(iv) Which of the following is a natural fertiliser?

    (a) Neem leaves   (b) Soil

    (c) Earthworm   (d) Cowdung

4. Read a newspaper report and answer the following questions.

Tuesday, 18th December, 2007, Andhra Pradesh

Farmers in Andhra Pradesh have been sent to jail for not being able to pay back their loans. They had suffered a big loss in farming. One of these farmers, Nallappa Reddy, had taken a bank loan of ₹24,000. To repay the loan, he had to take another loan from a private moneylender, at a very high rate of interest. Even after repaying ₹34,000 Reddy could not repay the entire loan. Reddy says, "The bank sends farmers to jail for not paying back small loans. But what about the big businessmen? They take loans of crores of rupees. Nothing happens to them when they do not return the money!".

Nallappa Reddy's story is shared by thousands of farmers in India who are suffering huge losses. The situation is so bad that many farmers see no way out of this except to commit suicide. According to government figures 150000 farmers have died like this between 1997 and 2005. This number may be much higher .....

(i) From which area is the report collected?

____

(ii) Why did farmers have to take loans?

____

(iii) Who are moneylenders? Why do they take a high rate of interest?

____

(iv) Farmers are sent to jail if they do not repay a small loan; however big businessmen who take loans of crores of rupees and do not repay their loan are excused. Why this discrimination is common in our country?

____

(v) Why do a large number of farmers commit suicide?

____

Very Short Answer Type Questions

5. Answer the following questions about when the pattern of farming changed in the village.

(i) What are the changes in the method of irrigation?

(ii) What type of crops are grown now?

(iii) What type of fertilisers are used?

(iv) What was used to keep away the insects?

(v) Why is there a little profit in farming now?

Short Answer Type Questions

6. Answer the following questions based on farming in earlier times.

(i) How did people celebrate when there was a good crop?

(ii) Why did farmers store a few seeds from a good crop? How did they store them?

(iii) What is *undhiya*? How was it prepared? How was it served?

(iv) What kind of crops were grown is earlier times?

(v) What kind of fertilisers were used by the farmers then?

(vi) Did they grow the same crop or different crops the whole year?

7. Answer the following questions in brief.

(i) Why did Hasmukh say, "Now we are farming wisely"?

(ii) What do you think was the disadvantage of replacing cows and buffaloes with a tractor?

(iii) How did the expenses of Hasmukh in farming increase?

(iv) Why did Paresh not want to do farming? What did he become then?

(v) Why was Paresh asking for the wooden seed box?

(vi) How does the following affect the soil?

(a) Fertilisers from factories.

(b) Medicines sprayed to keep away insects.

(vii) How did Pravin's uncle get good fertiliser without spending extra money?

(viii) Why are earthworms called 'soil's best friend'?

Long Answer Type Question

8. Answer in detail.
How was Hasmukh's way of farming different from that of Damjibhai?

Think, Find and Write

9. Arrange the following pictures in correct order of the journey of *bajra* seeds from field to plate.

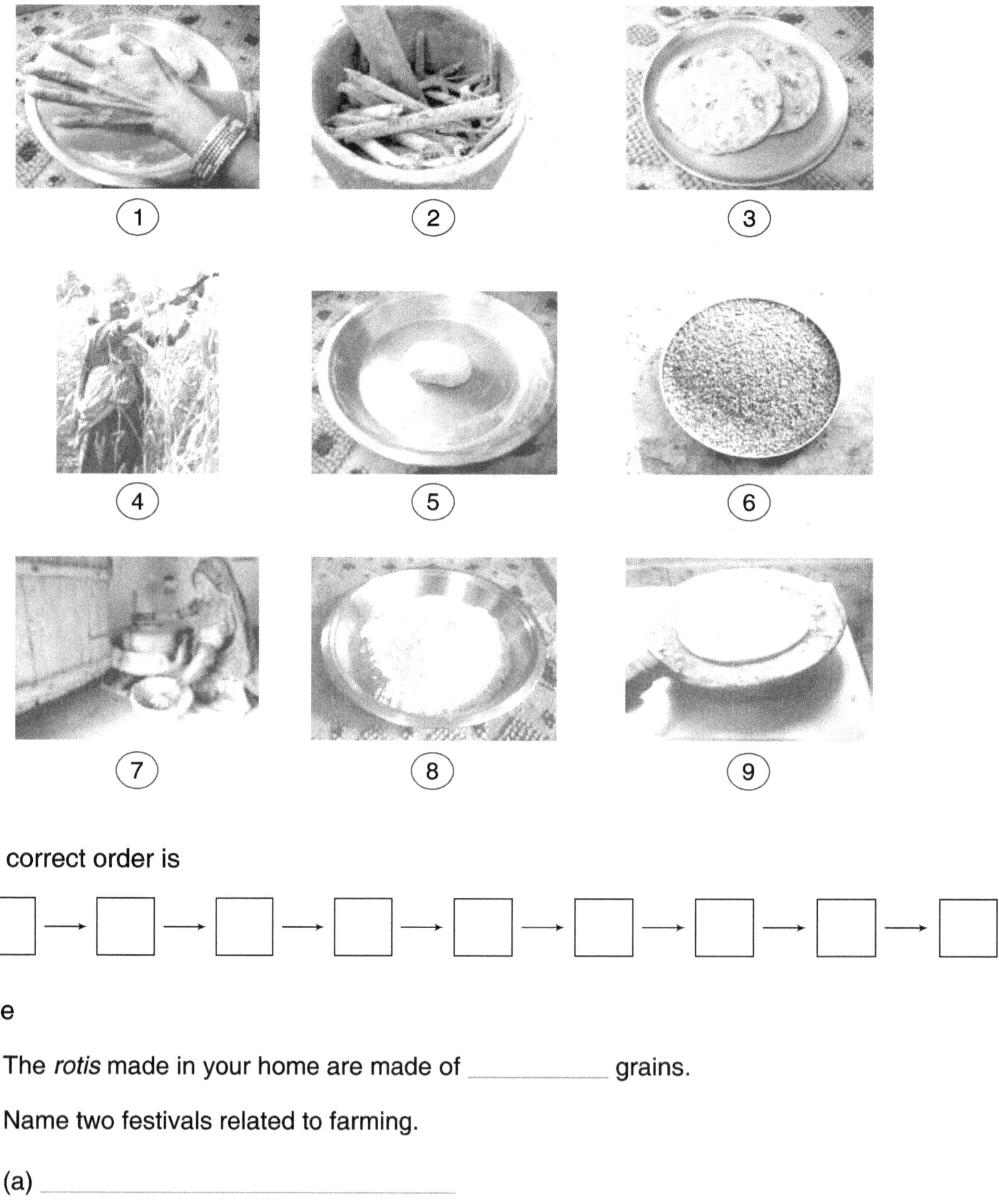

The correct order is

☐ → ☐ → ☐ → ☐ → ☐ → ☐ → ☐ → ☐ → ☐

10. Write

(i) The *rotis* made in your home are made of _____________ grains.

(ii) Name two festivals related to farming.

(a) _______________________________________

(b) _______________________________________

11. Write a short note on 'ill effects of changes in the pattern of farming'.

____

____

____

____

12. Match the following agricultural implements with the processes in which they are used.

Agricultural Implements	Processes
	Threshing
	Ploughing
	Sowing
	Harvesting
	Irrigation

Chapter 20

Whose Forests?

1. Fill in the blanks.

(i) Every ___________ Suryamani takes children to the forest.

(ii) To learn to read the forest is as important as reading a ___________ .

(iii) Suryamani passed her ___________ after getting a ___________ .

(iv) 'Torang' means jungle in ___________ language.

(v) Ash makes the land ___________ .

(vi) The main crop of Jhoom farming is ___________ .

2. Write 'T' for True and 'F' for False statements.

(i) The school in Bishanpur was near thick forest.

(ii) Suryamani was 31 when she opened her centre 'Torang'.

(iii) Mizoram is located in a coastal area.

(iv) In Jhoom farming, different crops can be grown on the same farm.

(v) In Mizoram very few children go to school.

3. Multiple Choice Questions (MCQs).

(i) To which community did Suryamani belong?

(a) Kuduk   (b) Baiga

(c) Bhils   (d) Khasis

(ii) Suryamani was associated with which movement?

(a) Chipko Movement   (b) Jharkhand Jungle Bachao Andolan

(c) Apiko Movement   (d) Narmada Bachao Andolan

(iii) To which state did Suryamani belong?

(a) Chhattisgarh   (b) Orissa

(c) Jharkhand   (d) Mizoram

(iv) What was the name of Suryamani's centre?

    (a) Kuduk   (b) Torang

    (c) Jungle Bachao   (d) Cheraw

(v) In Mizoram how much of the people are linked to forests?

    (a) 25%   (b) 40%

    (c) 50%   (d) 75%

4. Forests give us many products. Circle the ones which are obtained from forests.

Timber	*Coins*	*Milk*		
	Plastic	*Paper*	*Bamboo*	
Wool	*Herbs*	*Cotton*		*Wax*
	Spices	*Polythene*	*Medicine*	

Name some other products that we obtain from forests.

____

5. Read a part of the letter written by Sikhya a class X girl in Odisha to the Chief Minister and answer the questions that follows.

A forest is everything for us adivasis. We can't live away from the forests even for a day. Government has started many projects in the name of development - dams and factories are being built. Forests, which are ours, are being taken away from us. Because of these projects, we need to think where will the forest people go and what will happen to their livelihood? Where will the lakhs of animals living in the forests go? If there are no forests, and we dig our lands for minerals like aluminium, what will be left? Only polluted air, water, and miles and miles of barren land.

(i) How are adivasis dependent on forests?

____

(ii) What types of projects are started in the name of development?

____

(iii) How will these projects affect the forests, forest people and animals?

____

(iv) What will happen if forests disappear?

____

Very Short Answer Type Questions

6. Answer the following questions in one sentence.

(i) Why did Suryamani go to school?

(ii) What did Suryamani's father do?

(iii) What did Suryamani's mother do?

Short Answer Type Questions

7. Answer the following questions briefly.

(i) Why could the adivasis not take anything from the forest after the contractor came?

(ii) Why did Suryamani's father move to the town? How did Suryamani's *chacha* help them?

(iii) Why did Suryamani not want to study in the school in Bishanpur in the beginning?

(iv) Why did Suryamani's *chacha* want Suryamani to study in the school in Bishanpur?

(v) Why was Suryamani filled with joy later on when she saw the school at Bishanpur?

(vi) What is the 'girl stars' project?

(vii) Why are forest dwellers known as adivasis?

(viii) Why was Budhiyamai not scared of the contractor? Why did she say, "The forest is like our collective bank"?

(ix) Who was

    (a) Vasavi *didi?* _________________________

    (b) Bijoy? _________________________

    (c) Mirchi? _________________________

(x) How did Vasavi *didi* and Bijoy help Suryamani?

(xi) Why did Suryamani's father did not like Suryamani to work for the movement (to save forests)?

(xii) What was Suryamani's dream? With whom did she share her thoughts and dreams?

(xiii) Who are adivasis? For what right of adivasis was Suryamani fighting?

Long Answer Type Questions

8. Look at the picture and answer the following questions.

(i) Where are the children in the picture going?

(ii) In which language do they speak?

(iii) What do they do in the forest?

9. Answer the following questions based on the lottery system of farming followed in Mizoram.

   (i) How is the land allotted to village people for farming?

   (ii) Who allots these lands?

   (iii) What is the standard unit used to measure the land? Why is it called so?

10. Answer the following questions based on Jhoom farming.

   (i) How is Jhoom farming done? Where is such type of farming done?

   (ii) How is land made fertile in Jhoom farming?

   (iii) While burning bamboo or weeds, what care should be taken?

   (iv) How all crops are grown?

(v) The main crop is rice. Why is it difficult to take the crop home?

______

______

(vi) How do village people celebrate if they have a good crop? If some family is not able to do farming, then how do other people help that family?

______

______

(vii) Which is their special dance? How is it carried out?

______

______

Think, Find and Write

11. Explain the following terms.

Deforestation ______

Afforestation ______

12. Name any two

(i) Things made of bamboo

(a) ______   (b) ______

(ii) Movements to save forests

(a) ______   (b) ______

13. Write in brief about "The Right to Forest Act, 2007".

______

______

14. What effect does the cutting down of forests have on the environment? What can you do to protect your environment?

______

______

Chapter 21

Like Father, Like Daughter

1. Fill in the blanks.

(i) Some traits or habits we get from our ____________ whereas some habits and skills are learnt from our ____________ .

(ii) An ____________ child does not resemble the people who bring it up.

(iii) ____________ are affected when a person suffers from polio.

(iv) ____________ explained the transfer of traits to the next generation using pea plant.

2. Write 'T' for True and 'F' for False statements.

(i) Two sisters brought up in different environments behave in a similar way.

(ii) Polio can be transferred from parents to their children.

(iii) Mendel did not have money to study at university.

(iv) Our abilities may change because of some illness or old age.

Short Answer Type Questions

3. Answer the following questions based on Mendel and his experiment.

(i) When and where was Mendel born?

(ii) What was his father's occupation?

(iii) Was Mendel fond of studies?

(iv) What did Mendel want to become?

(v) Why did Mendel always keep failing in his exams?

(vi) Why did Mendel become a monk?

(vii) Where and on which plant did Mendel do his experiment?

(viii) What did Mendel discover through his experiments?

4. Answer the following questions in brief.

(i) Give two examples of problems that are age related or acquired due to old age.

(ii) What factors contribute in making our identity?

(iii) Which part of the body is affected by polio? Is this hereditary?

5. Answer the following questions about twins.

(i) Who are twins?

(ii) Write their similarities.

(iii) How are they different?

Long Answer Type Questions

6. Why do we sneeze?

7. How can polio be prevented? What efforts are government making to eradicate polio from our country?

8. What values does our family teach us?

9. What are traits? List some traits that you have inherited from your parents.

10. Write some factors that are inherited by birth and some factors that are not.

Think, Find and Write

11. Answer the following questions about you and your family.

    (i) What is the colour of your eyes?

    (ii) What is the colour of your hair? How long are your hair?

    (iii) What is your height?

    (iv) Does your face or anything else look similar to that of someone else in your family? With whom you have similarity?

    (v) Are any of your habits or traits similar to your father? Which ones?

(vi) Are any of your habits or traits similar to your mother? Which ones?

____

(vii) Are any of your habits or traits similar to any other person in the family? With whom? Which ones?

____

12. Find the meaning of the following words.

(i) Hereditary ____

(ii) Trait ____

(iii) Siblings ____

(iv) Adoption ____

13. Find out and write

(i) The names of any two diseases which can be transferred from parents to their children.

______________________________   ______________________________

(ii) The names of any two diseases which are not transferred from parents to their children.

______________________________   ______________________________

14. Draw your family tree.

Chapter 22

On The Move Again

1. Fill in the blanks with appropriate words given in the box.

> motor, 3 months, paddy, caravan, ill, young, 6 months, sugarcane, old, study, play

(i) Mukadam is an agent for _____________ factories.

(ii) For _____________ Dhanu and many children like him will not be able to go to school.

(iii) _____________ and _____________ people stayed back in the village.

(iv) The _____________ of families would settle near sugarcane fields and factories.

(v) If children _____________ they can become good person in life and have a better future.

2. Write 'T' for True and 'F' for False statements.

(i) Mukadam is an agent who lends money. ☐

(ii) Farming is not possible without rain. ☐

(iii) Dhanu was not fond of studies. ☐

(iv) Near a sugarcane field people live in huts made of dry sugarcane and its leaves. ☐

(v) Dhanu helps his father in sugarcane fields. ☐

3. Answer the following questions based on Dussehra celebration in Dhanu's village.

(i) Who all have come to Dhanu's house?

(ii) Why have they come to Dhanu's house?

____

(iii) What things have Dhanu's mother and aunt prepared?

____

(iv) Why did everybody's mood change in the evening? What did they do in the evening?

____

4. Answer the following questions based on evening meeting on Dussehra in Dhanu's village?

(i) Why was a meeting held on Dussehra evening? What did the Mukadam tell the village people?

____

(ii) Where did the village people work before and after Dussehra?

____

(iii) Why did the village people have to borrow money from the Mukadam?

____

5. Answer the following questions based on moving to the new place.

(i) Who all will go with Dhanu's family to the new place?

____

(ii) Will all the members of Dhanu's family go with him? Why?

____

(iii) What problems will Dhanu and his family members have to face due to shifting?

____

6. Answer the following questions based on life after Dussehra. Dhanu's family and many other families have settled near the sugarcane fields and sugar factories after Dussehra.

(i) Where will Dhanu's family stay? Do they have a house near the sugar factory?

____

(ii) Does Dhanu go to school at the new place? Why?

____

(iii) What work do men and women have to do in sugar factories? Do they get enough money?

____

(iv) How long will they stay near the sugar factory?

____

(v) Do children also work in the fields and factories? Why?

____

(vi) For what did the workers get a receipt in the factory?

____

(vii) What did Dhanu's *aai* and *mami* buy from the money they got?

____

Think, Find and Write

7. Define the following terms in one sentence each.

    (i) Caravan

    (ii) Migration

    (iii) Debts

    (iv) Loan

    (v) Agent

8. Write a few lines on each topic.

    (i) The problems, a family and its children have to face when they move from one place to the other.

    (ii) Common problems of farmers in India.

    (iii) How can arrangements be made for educating children of communities that are on the move?

9. Name a few communities who have to migrate from one place to another for work.

    (i)   (ii)

    (iii)   (iv)

10. The role of Mukadam in the life of poor village people.

<u>Answers</u>

Chapter 1   Super Senses

1. (i) smell   (ii) Mosquitoes   (iii) 4   (iv) sloths   (v) hunters, poachers
2. (i) F   (ii) F   (iii) F   (iv) F   (v) T   (vi) F
3. (i) (b)   (ii) (c)   (iii) (c)   (iv) (d)   (v) (c)
4. (i) smell   (ii) see   (iii) smell   (iv) hear   (v) feel   (vi) smell
5. (i) (d)   (ii) (a)   (iii) (e)   (iv) (c)   (v) (b)
6. (i) (d)   (ii) (a)   (iii) (b)   (iv) (c)   (v) (e)

Chapter 2   A Snake Charmer's Story

1. (i) Kalbeliyas, *been*   (ii) medicines   (iii) mark   (iv) death   (v) fangs
2. (i) T   (ii) T   (iii) T   (iv) F   (v) T
3. (i) (d)   (ii) (a)   (iii) (a)   (iv) (b)   (v) (c)
4. (i) Cobra   (ii) Duboiya   (iii) Krait   (iv) Afai

Chapter 3   From Tasting to Digesting

1. (i) Cooked vegetables   (ii) Jaggery   (iii) Tamarind   (iv) Bitter gourd
2. (i) chew   (ii) sugar,salt   (iii) glucose   (iv) Beaumont   (v) proper food

Chapter 4   Mangoes Round the Year

1. (i) Milk   (ii) Onion   (iii) ripe   (iv) muslin   (v) fridge/refrigerator   (vi) sugar
2. (i) (c)   (ii) (b)   (iii) (c)   (iv) (a)   (v) (b)

Chapter 5   Seeds and Seeds

1. (i) sprouted   (ii) air, water, warmth   (iii) George Mestral
    (iv) bursting, pods   (v) Europe
2. (i) T   (ii) T   (iii) T   (iv) T
3. (i) (d)   (ii) (a)   (iii) (b)   (iv) (b)

Chapter 6   Every Drop Counts

1. (i) lake   (ii) stepwells   (iii) celebrate   (iv) necessity   (v) Rain
2. (i) T   (ii) F   (iii) F   (iv) T   (v) T
3. (i) (d)   (ii) (c)   (iii) (b)   (iv) (d)   (v) (c)

Chapter 7   Experiment With Water

1. (i) sinks   (ii) Dead   (iii) Honey   (iv) salt   (v) Sea water
2. (i) F   (ii) F   (iii) T   (iv) T   (v) F   (vi) F   (vii) T
3. (i) (d)   (ii) (d)   (iii) (c)   (iv) (c)   (v) (b)   (vi) (b)

Chapter 8   A Treat For Mosquitoes

1. (i) Anopheles   (ii) Dengue, *Chikungunya*   (iii) Algae
   (iv) Flies   (v) Ronald Ross
2. (i) T   (ii) F   (iii) T   (iv) T   (v) T   (vi) T
   (vii) T   (viii) F   (ix) T
3. (i) (a)   (ii) (d)   (iii) (c)   (iv) (b)   (v) (d)   (vi) (b)   (vii) (b)

Chapter 9   Up You Go

1. (i) blisters   (ii) Mizo   (iii) pegs   (iv) 90°   (v) cucumbers
   (vi) sticks   (vii) Sangeeta   (viii) Bachhendri Pal, 5th   (ix) 8848
2. (i) T   (ii) F   (iii) T   (iv) F   (v) T   (vi) T

Chapter 10   Walls Tell Stories

1. (i) Qutubshahi   (ii) nuclear   (iii) Fateh Darwaza   (iv) Clay   (v) carvings
2. (i) F   (ii) T   (iii) F   (iv) T   (v) T
3. (i) (c)   (ii) (c)   (iii) (d)   (iv) (d)   (v) (b)
5. (i) Bastions   (ii) Cannon   (iii) Mehrab   (iv) Museum   (v) Mashak

Chapter 11   Sunita in Space

1. (i) seas and oceans   (ii) blobs   (iii) 6 months   (iv) land, sea
2. (i) F   (ii) T   (iii) T   (iv) F   (v) F
3. (i) (b)   (ii) (d)   (iii) (c)   (iv) (e)   (v) (c)

Chapter 12   What if it Finishes?

1. (i) Ahmedabad   (ii) bicycle   (iii) petrol pump   (iv) Switch off   (v) pipes, machines   (vi) damp
2. (i) T   (ii) T   (iii) T   (iv) T
   (v) F   (vi) F   (vii) T   (viii) T
3. (i) (b)   (ii) (c)   (iii) (d)   (iv) (b)   (v) (c)

Chapter 13   A Shelter So High

1. (i) loner   (ii) 1400   (iii) Mumbai   (iv) Ladakh   (v) welcome   (vi) houseboat
   (vii) 80, 8   (viii) donga   (ix) Mehraab
2. (i) F   (ii) T   (iii) T   (iv) F   (v) F
   (vi) F   (vii) T
3. (i) (c)   (ii) (b)   (iii) (c)   (iv) (c)   (v) (a)   (vi) (b)

Chapter 14   When the Earth Shook

1. (i) fractured   (ii) 6   (iii) Cold, fear   (iv) Scientists   (v) Engineers, Architects   (vi) lie down
2. (i) F   (ii) F   (iii) F   (iv) T   (v) F
3. (i) (c)   (ii) (d)   (iii) (b)   (iv) (c)

Chapter 15   Blow Hot, Blow Cold

1. (i) moisture   (ii) goes in, comes out   (iii) Hot   (iv) Cool

2. (i) T   (ii) T   (iii) T   (iv) F   (v) F

Chapter 16   Who Will Do This Work?

2. (i) T   (ii) T   (iii) T   (iv) F   (v) T   (vi) T

Chapter 17   Across The Wall

1. (i) district   (ii) player   (iii) injured   (iv) Cooperation (v) speak, best   (vi) everyone

2. (i) T   (ii) F   (iii) F   (iv) T   (v) T   (vi) T

3. (i) (b)   (ii) (c)   (iii) (a)   (iv) (b)   (v) (c)

Chapter 18   No Place for Us

1. (i) Khedi   (ii) unwanted guests   (iii) Khedi, Sinduri, Mumbai   (iv) dam   (v) school

2. (i) T   (ii) T   (iii) T   (iv) F   (v) T   (vi) F   (vii) F

Chapter 19   A Seed Tells a Farmer's Story

1. (i) *bajra*   (ii) fresh   (iii) *charkha*   (iv) Electricity   (v) tractor

2. (i) F   (ii) F   (iii) F   (iv) T   (v) T

3. (i) (c)   (ii) (d)   (iii) (c)   (iv) (d)

Chapter 20   Whose Forests?

1. (i) Sunday   (ii) book   (iii) BA, scholarship   (iv) Kuduk   (v) fertile   (vi) rice

2. (i) T   (ii) F   (iii) F   (iv) T   (v) F

3. (i) (a)   (ii) (b)   (iii) (c)   (iv) (b)   (v) (d)

Chapter 21   Like Father, Like Daughter

1. (i) family, environment   (ii) adopted   (iii) Legs   (iv) Mendel

2. (i) F   (ii) F   (iii) T   (iv) T

Chapter 22   On The Move Again

1. (i) Sugarcane   (ii) 6 months   (iii) Old, ill   (iv) caravan   (v) study

2. (i) T   (ii) F   (iii) T   (iv) T   (v) T